WHY COMMUNITY LAND TRUSTS?

A Common Ground Monograph

WHY COMMUNITY LAND TRUSTS?

The Philosophy Behind an
Unconventional Form of Tenure

John Emmeus Davis
Line Algoed
María E. Hernández-Torrales

EDITORS

TERRA NOSTRA PRESS
Madison, Wisconsin, USA

TERRA NOSTRA PRESS

Center for Community Land Trust Innovation
3146 Buena Vista Street
Madison, Wisconsin, USA 53704

Publisher's Cataloging-in-Publication Data

Names: Davis, John Emmeus, editor. | Algoed, Line, editor. | Hernández-Torrales, María E., editor.
Title: Why community land trusts? The philosophy behind an unconventional form of tenure. / John Emmeus Davis ; Line Algoed ; María E. Hernández-Torrales, editors.
Series: Common Ground Monographs
Description: Includes bibliographical references. | Madison, WI: Terra Nostra Press, 2020.
Identifiers: Library of Congress Control Number: 2020907975 |
ISBN 978-1-7344030-4-6 (paperback) | ISBN: 978-1-7344030-6-0 (ebook)
Subjects: LCSH Land trusts. | Land tenure. | Land use. | Land use, Urban. | Nature conservation. | Landscape protection. | Sustainable development. | Sustainable development—Developing countries. | Economic development—Environmental aspects. | City planning—Environmental aspects. | Community development. | Urban ecology (Sociology) | BISAC POLITICAL SCIENCE / Public Policy / City Planning & Urban Development | LAW / Housing & Urban Development | BUSINESS & ECONOMICS / Development / Sustainable Development | SOCIAL SCIENCE / Sociology / Urban
Classification: LCC KF736.L3 W49 2020 | DDC 333.2—dc23

CONTENTS

FIGURES

Foreword

Jerry Maldonado
FORD FOUNDATION

As a social justice foundation committed to the advancement of human dignity, the Ford Foundation has prioritized the reduction of inequality as a central, unifying goal across its diverse program areas. While most debates on inequality focus narrowly on the ways in which income and wealth disparities have dramatically increased over the past few decades, less attention is typically paid to the ways in which inequality is often hardwired into the built environment.

In cities and regions across the globe, housing, land use and infrastructure decisions have often accelerated, reinforced and sustained the physical, economic and social disparities that divide communities. Discriminatory land use, housing and urban development policies have perpetuated racial and economic segregation. In the United States, the country's massive racial wealth gap was built on the back of racially exclusive housing and land use practices that systematically restricted the ability of African-Americans, Latinos, and other communities of color to build assets through the ownership of land and housing. Urban renewal, redlining and the construction of the country's federal highway system targeted low-income communities of color, stripping them of their assets, and laying the foundation for today's highly segregated physical and social landscape.

Structural racism, segregation and market fundamentalism are a toxic mix. Together, they have produced one of the most radically unequal global economies of our time, concentrating economic and political power in fewer and fewer private hands at enormous cost to our fragile planet and our shared humanity. Today, millions of people across the globe—from New York to Puerto Rico, from Johannesburg to Rio de Janeiro—have been systematically deprived of their basic human rights to decent housing, work and other essential services, while corporate profits have soared. Sadly, our rapidly escalating global housing and displacement crisis represents just the latest incarnation of a broader boom-bust, predatory real estate investment and development cycle that continues to actively marginalize countless communities. These growing economic and physical divides are neither morally nor politically sustainable.

But inequality is not inevitable. It is the result of conscious decisions, policies and politics that perpetuate a culture of scarcity and competition. It's fueled by extractive economic development policies that too often exploit workers, land and communities in pursuit of short-term profits. As such, the contestation over land, development and housing can be viewed as part of a broader struggle over power and the future of our democracies. Who decides and who benefits from development? Who belongs and who is excluded? Whose history and culture is valued and whose is rendered invisible? The choices we make around land use and housing reflect our collective answers to these questions. As such, they are fundamentally moral decisions—reflections on which communities are "valued" and which are deemed "expendable."

In this moment of extreme global polarization, it is more urgent than ever that we find a new, COMMON GROUND that recalibrates and rebalances the relationship between the market, government and civil society. Over the last several decades, community-based organizations across the globe—a number of which are in this monograph—have not only challenged exclusionary housing and development practices, but have also demonstrated that another way is possible. From the Champlain Housing

> The CLT movement is unique in the way that it centers housing and land as part of a broader movement for community self-determination.

Trust (Vermont), to the Dudley Street Neighborhood Initiative (Boston), to the Fideicomiso de La Tierra in El Caño Martín Peña (Puerto Rico), organized leaders and communities have pioneered innovative models of inclusive development that have helped revitalize distressed communities, prevent forced evictions, and promote land security and stability. The community land trust movement is unique in the way that it centers housing and land as part of a broader movement for community self-determination. At their best, community land trusts not only function as tools for preventing displacement and preserving long-term affordability, but also as vehicles for collective deliberation, action and accountability that help to bend the arc of development toward justice.

The visionary leaders, communities and organizations featured in this monograph are at the forefront of a broader national and global movement attempting to recalibrate the relationship between governments and markets in housing and development policy. Significantly, many of the case studies in this book highlight the critical role that the public sector can and must play in order to significantly scale up these community-led interventions. National, state and local governments all have an important role to play in creating the right land use, housing and investment policies that not only constrain some of the market's worst excesses, but also harness development in a way that preserves public resources and assets in perpetuity for the common good.

Helen Keller once famously argued that "the heresy of one age becomes the orthodoxy of the next." It is our hope that the lessons, insights, struggles and victories captured in this monograph challenge and inspire policymakers, advocates and community leaders around the globe to reimagine the relationship between people, communities and land in a way that centers human dignity, shared prosperity and the long-term stewardship of our natural assets.

—

David Ireland
WORLD HABITAT

What makes good housing? Read the adverts in glossy magazines and you might be led to think that people aspire to glassy high-rise apartments with swanky roof terraces and all the latest designer gadgetry. Speak to ordinary people and the answer is very different.

This monograph proposes an answer to that question. It examines the philosophy behind the growth and global spread of one of the most important ideas of the last century—the community land trust. It describes how communities in very different contexts have adapted and are using the community land trust model to change the way land is owned, create new homes and protect their community. Ultimately it allows ordinary people to lead happier lives.

The World Happiness Report is a global annual survey measuring people's general happiness. It identifies several factors that make people most happy about where they live. It cites family support and security, personal health, the freedom to make choices, people's generosity, and a perception of fairness and the absence of corruption.

Most people spend around half of their lives in and around their home. Good housing is perhaps the single most important factor in ensuring people lead happy, healthy and fulfilled lives. Housing is the backdrop to our lives. It's where our family life takes place, where we come home to after being at school or work. It's where we become part of a community. It becomes part of our identity. It's where we're from. It's where we call home.

Yet for an increasing number of people around the world, the very factors that make housing good are under threat. Global capital has moved into rented housing with devasting consequences for the people who live there. Leilani Farha, the UN Special Rapporteur on Housing Rights, calls it the "financialization of housing." From mass forced evictions to make way for luxury developments, to nameless corporations buying up real estate, to empty homes and people being pushed out of their communities because they simply cannot afford to live there, the repercussions are being felt across the globe.

Across most of the developed world, government-funded social or public housing was once available as a right for people who could not afford the cost of market housing. But austerity and a shift in political philosophy have caused much of this government-funded housing to be sold off and, for much that is left, its security has been watered down. In many countries, the poorest are left to fend for themselves at the bottom end of the private market. Forced into overcrowded and often insanitary accommodation, some are driven into homelessness.

The Climate Emergency is harming the places that many people live. Rising temperatures, droughts, wildfires, hurricanes, and floods are making the places many poorer communities live more dangerous and unhealthy. The future for some communities is bleak as they watch their homeland become uninhabitable.

If people's legal rights are weakened, if the private market is more hostile, and if nature itself is so damaged that it reacts against us, who can we turn to; who will protect us and our homes? The answer is our community.

The community land trust, along with other forms of community-led housing, is a powerful response, based on the simple principle that people are stronger when they work together. Their strength is magnified when they collectively control the land on which their housing is built. Community-owned land and community-led development go hand-in-hand in the community land trust, providing the legal muscle to resist threats from predatory land developers and the financial strength to insulate people from the affordability jeopardy caused by financialization. It also gives communities the strength to commission and design better homes that meet people's needs and that are capable of withstanding the dangers wreaked by an increasingly unpredictable climate.

> Communities are given the strength to shape their own destiny; individuals are given the freedom to lead their own lives.

The community land trust movement has taken those principles and enshrined them in a set of simple rules for structuring an organization and for structuring the tenure of land and housing. These rules give communities the legal and financial strength to shape their own destiny, while allowing individual households the freedom to lead their own lives. The community land trust relies on a democratic model that gives people a voice and a stake in their community. It's a compelling idea that provides an answer to an increasingly dysfunctional housing system and a less benign world.

Although community land trusts can trace their origins back many decades, it is almost as if they were invented just yesterday as a specific response to the problems of the modern world. It should be no surprise that the community land trust movement is growing and spreading. Its forms of organization and tenure are being recognised in law and the model itself is being adapted to different circumstances and cultures.

My own organisation has recognised and championed this growth and global spread. In 2008 we presented the World Habitat Award to the Champlain Housing Trust in Vermont, an early pioneer in a movement dedicated to creating homes that are affordable in perpetuity in real estate markets that are squeezing out lower- and middle-income earners. The Award helped the CLT concept to transfer across the Atlantic and inspired the first community land trust in Europe—founded in Brussels. We have continued to recognise the growth of the movement with Communauté Milton-Parc in Montreal, Canada, Tanzania-Bondeni in Kenya, Habitat para la Mujer in Bolivia, and Grandby Four Streets in Liverpool, UK. All of them receiving recognition in the World Habitat Awards.

I am particularly excited by the Fideicomiso de la Tierra del Caño Martín Peña in Puerto Rico which received the World Habitat Award in 2015. It has adapted the community land trust model to an informal settlement for the first time. Informal settlements are home to over a billion of the poorest people around the world. In the Caño Martín Peña, the community land trust has helped protect the community against the twin threats of predatory land speculation and flooding from a local watercourse. This innovation has the potential to pave the way for community land trusts to be adopted in other countries as a way of regularizing tenure and improving conditions in informal settlements, improving the lives of millions of people living in the most insecure and unsafe housing. The movement is spreading through Europe too, providing new options for communities in Eastern Europe where the mass privatization of state housing in the late 1980s left a distorted and inflexible housing market.

My own experience of visiting community land trusts around the world leaves me with many memories, but one overriding emotion: happiness. Every resident involved in creating a community land trust or lucky enough to live in a community land trust home has talked of how the land trust has improved their lives. Where they live, makes them happy. It's an unarguable endorsement of this form of housing and the best evidence of what good housing really is.

Why Community Land Trusts?
The Philosophy Behind an
Unconventional Form of Tenure

John Emmeus Davis, Line Algoed,
and María E. Hernández-Torrales

Fifty years ago, a group of visionary African-Americans who had led the struggle for voting rights and racial equality in Albany, Georgia established New Communities Inc., an organization later credited with being the first community land trust. These Civil Rights activists had come to believe that owning land was one of the keys to securing political and economic independence for their people. But landownership was out of reach for most African-Americans in the Deep South of the 1960s and too easily lost if they did acquire a small farm, a plot of land, or a house in town. The founders of New Communities concluded that *community* ownership by a not-for-profit, nongovernmental organization would be a more secure form of tenure. Community-owned land could be combined, moreover, with the *individual* ownership of newly built houses, offering low-income people an opportunity to become homeowners. In addition, community-owned land could provide a platform for the cooperative organization of farming and other enterprises, offering low-income people a chance for economic prosperity.

This ingenious hybrid, blending multiple owners and uses under the watchful eye of a community-controlled, nonprofit organization, was the prototype for what eventually became, after fine-tuning in subsequent years, the "community land trust" (CLT).

The earliest CLTs, like the one at New Communities, were started in rural areas. These organizations were often concerned as much with the cultivation of farmlands and the conservation of woodlands as they were with the production of housing. By the 1980s and 1990s, however, the focus of this fledgling CLT movement had shifted somewhat, as CLTs began proliferating in cities, suburbs, and towns. The concerns of these newer organizations were predictably urban: revitalizing the built environment in distressed neighborhoods; preventing the displacement of lower-income residents in gentrifying neighborhoods; and promoting the development of many different forms of affordable housing.

There are now over 260 community land trusts in the United States. But this "new model for land tenure in America," as it was originally called, is no longer exclusively — nor predominantly—"American." Over 300 CLTs are presently up and running in England and Wales. Others have been established in Australia, Belgium, Canada, and France. Interest has been rising in Germany, Ireland, Italy, the Netherlands, Portugal, Scotland, and Spain as well.

Although most CLT development to date has occurred in the Global North, that is changing. Interest is growing in the Global South, seeded by a high-impact CLT in Puerto Rico. This grassroots organization, the *Fideicomiso de la Tierra del Caño Martín Peña*, has made steady progress in regularizing land tenure and securing the homes of hundreds of families residing in informal settlements along a tidal channel in San Juan. The high-profile success of the Caño Martín Peña CLT has attracted the attention of people living in similar situations throughout Latin America and the Caribbean, wherever the lands and homes of lower-income people are insecure. Community activists working in informal settlements in Africa and South Asia have also taken note, exploring whether some version of the CLT might be used to promote equitable and sustainable development within their own countries.

On Common Ground: International Perspectives on the Community Land Trust, a collection of original essays published in June 2020, documented the emergence, diversification, and cross-pollination of this worldwide CLT movement. Most of the book's twenty-six chapters were devoted to answering such familiar journalistic questions as "who," "what," "when," "where," and "how." The unfolding stories of CLT pioneers, organizations, and strategies took center stage. But a number of chapters also addressed the question of "why," examining the philosophy behind this unconventional form of tenure. These were selected for the present monograph.

Included here are the six essays from *On Common Ground* that delved most deeply into the theoretical and practical justifications for the "ingenious hybrid" that is spreading slowly across the global landscape. Each makes its case for the CLT in a somewhat different way, giving precedence to one set of complementary arguments over another. Taken together, they provide a coherent and compelling rationale for why community land trusts are worthy of consideration, implementation, and support.

WHAT'S IN A NAME?

Community land trusts are not all alike. Among the hundreds of CLTs that already exist or are presently being planned, there are numerous variations in how these organizations are structured, how their lands are utilized, how development is done, and how the stewardship of housing is operationalized. What is called a "community land trust" can vary greatly from one country to another, even from one community to another within the same country.

The main features of the modern-day CLT were initially outlined in a book published in 1972. The book's authors based their blueprint on the unfolding experiment at New Communities Inc., but they also drew on a number of historical precedents. These included the collectively owned lands of indigenous peoples, the town commons of New England, the *moshav ovdim* of Israel, the *ejidos* of Mexico, the *Ujamaa Vijijini* of Tanzania, and the *Gramdan* villages of India.

The CLT model described in 1972 also resembled the mixed-ownership scheme that Ebenezer Howard had proposed in 1898 for his Garden Cities in England. The houses, stores, orchards, and factories in the new towns he proposed to establish on the outskirts of major cities would be privately owned by individuals, cooperatives, or for-profit businesses, but the underlying land would be owned forever by a nongovernmental organization, created expressly for that purpose. These scattered parcels of land would then be made available for planned development and productive use through long-term ground leases, executed between the nonprofit landowner and myriad individuals who owned buildings or operated enterprises on the leaseholds. Land was to be held and managed on behalf of *all* residents — rich and poor, present and future — enabling a community to direct its own development, to determine its own fate, and to capture for the common good a majority of the gains in land value that society as a whole had helped to create.

To the mixed-ownership model pioneered in England, India, and elsewhere, the founders of New Communities — and the reflective practitioners who followed in their wake — added organizational and operational features of their own, turning the model into something different, something new. Community-owned land remained the foundation on which a CLT was to be established, with a private, nonprofit corporation holding and managing scattered parcels of land for the benefit of residents of a particular locale, especially low-income families in need of housing. What got *added* were mechanisms for ensuring that the development done by a CLT would be guided by the community, as would the organization itself. This was not development from above, dictated by a governmental body, a charitable investor, or a benevolent provider of social housing. It was development from below, directed by residents of the community that a CLT had been organized to serve. Ownership and empowerment went hand-in-hand.

Added, too, was an operational commitment to the stewardship of any lands entrusted to the CLT and of any buildings erected on its lands, most of which would be owned by somebody else. Projects pursued by a CLT were designed to ensure that housing, nonresidential buildings, and other land uses would remain continuously affordable, long after development was done.

These distinctive features of ownership, organization, and operation, overlapping and interacting in a dynamic model of place-based development, became eventually known

COMMUNITY
(Organization)

LAND
(Ownership)

TRUST
(Operation)

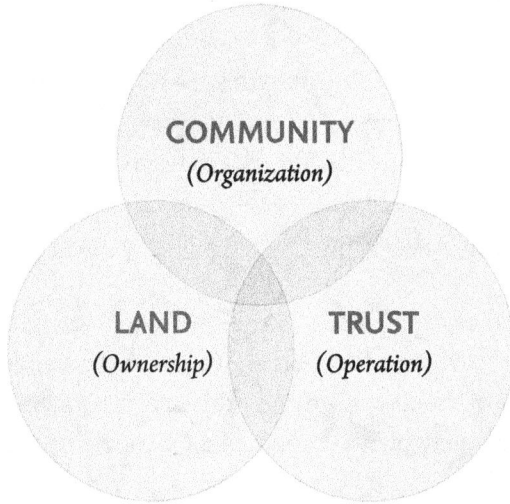

as the "classic" CLT. Almost as soon as nearly everyone came to agree on this particular conception and configuration of the community land trust, however, the model began to be modified in countless ways. Variations arose in every feature of the "classic" CLT, as practitioners in different places adapted it to fit conditions, needs, and priorities in their own communities or to fit customs and laws in their own countries.

This continuing process of innovation and adaptation has helped the CLT to spread across a disparate international landscape and to thrive in a range of settings. At the same time, the diversity of meanings attached to the model and the variety of ways in which CLTs are structured has introduced a degree of difficulty to the task of explaining exactly what a CLT might be. Today, there is ambiguity — even a dose of controversy — to be found in the description and implementation of every component.

Community. Throughout the world, most organizations that call themselves a CLT are committed to involving a place-based population in their activities, incorporating a participatory ethos into their organization's purposes, practices, and structure. People who live on the CLT's lands and those who live nearby are encouraged to become voting members of the organization. They are recruited to serve on its governing board.[1] They are invited to participate in shaping the uses and projects proposed by the CLT. Development is "community-led," along with the organization that initiates and oversees that development.

Ambiguity enters the picture because of the varying arrangements that CLTs employ in striving to engage and to empower their community. Controversy arises because some CLTs have dispensed with community altogether, causing critics to question whether they should even be considered a "real" CLT. The traditional model's distinctive features of ownership and operation might be present, but residents who are served by the program neither govern nor guide it; "community" is missing from the organizational make-up of the entity doing development. Variations like these create perennial challenges for CLT advocates whenever they try to reach a consensus as to what deserves to be deemed a "community land trust."[2]

Land. The typical CLT is a nonprofit organization that removes land permanently from the marketplace, managing it on behalf of a place-based community while making it available for long-term use by individuals and organizations. Title to the buildings on a CLTs land, either those existing when the CLT acquired the land or those constructed later on, is held individually by any number of parties – homeowners, cooperatives, businesses, gardeners, farmers, etc. The underlying land is leased from the CLT by the buildings' owners.

This mixed-ownership arrangement blurs the legal and conceptual boundary between conventional categories of tenure, where real property is presumed to be one thing or the other. A community land trust messes up this tidy picture, for it is balanced half-way between the two extremes of *individual property*, owned and operated primarily for the purpose of promoting private interests; and *collective property*, owned and operated to promote a common interest. The CLT tilts toward the former in its treatment of buildings. It tilts toward the latter in its treatment of land, making the CLT a first cousin to cooperatives, co-housing, and various forms of communal, collective, and tribal land.

A CLT's lands are frequently and fairly characterized as "community-owned" or, in the parlance of the series of which this monograph is a part, as "common ground." But these landholdings are neither collectively nor cooperatively owned by the people living on them or around them. Title is held exclusively by the CLT. A community land trust is ownership for the common good, not ownership in common.[3]

There are places, however, where the separation of ownership is made difficult (or impossible) by quirks in the property laws of a particular country or by the quibbles of prospective funders. CLTs have sometimes been compelled, therefore, to retain ownership of buildings as well as the land or to relinquish ownership of both, while imposing long-lasting restrictions on the use and affordability of these properties. Another variation has been developed in Puerto Rico, where the Caño Martín Peña CLT holds the underlying land but uses a durable surface rights deed, rather than a ground lease, to provide security of tenure for people who own and occupy houses on the CLT's land. Some of these residents are living on sites their families have occupied for nearly a hundred years.

Trust. Although "trust" is part of their given name, CLTs have rarely been established as real estate trusts.[4] Most are NGOs – that is, private, nonprofit corporations with a charitable purpose of meeting the needs of populations who are regularly underserved by both the market and the state. "Trust" refers not to how a CLT is organized, but to how it is operated. "Trust" is what a CLT *does* in overseeing the lands and buildings under its care and in performing the duties of stewardship. Foremost among these duties is the preservation of affordability, ensuring long-term access to land and housing for people of modest means and preventing their displacement due to gentrification and other pressures. Stewardship also includes such responsibilities as preventing deferred maintenance in housing and other buildings on the CLT's land and intervening, if necessary, to protect occupants against predatory lending, arbitrary eviction, mortgage foreclosure, and other threats to security of tenure. Some CLTs are focused less on the provision of housing, however, than on the preservation of watersheds, woodlands, or agricultural lands, either in rural or urban areas. The stewardship responsibilities of a CLT entrusted with managing such lands can look very different than the stewardship needed when affordable housing is a CLT's operational focus.

WHAT DO CLTS HAVE IN COMMON?

Despite this lack of uniformity in the description, implementation, and application of CLTs, there are commonalities nonetheless. What unites a global community of CLT scholars and practitioners is more important than what separates us. There is a *lingua franca* for understanding what it means for an organization to be a CLT and to behave like one. There is a shared commitment to reinventing and repurposing real estate for the common good. There is a shared conviction that community-owned land, in particular, is likely to do a better job of promoting equitable and sustainable development than land that is commodified and owned individually, especially in places populated by groups that have long been disadvantaged and disempowered.

Another trait shared by most CLT scholars and practitioners is a conviction that the whole of a CLT is greater than the sum of its parts. Across the diverse landscape of CLTs, ownership, organization, and operation are not configured exactly the same in every town and country. Wherever this strategy has been adopted, however, there is a general recognition that it takes more than a single component to make a CLT; it takes more than the reinvention of any one of them to bend the arc of development toward a fairer distribution of property and power. Community-owned land, by itself, is not enough. Community-led development is not enough. Permanently affordable housing is not enough. It is their *combination* that gives a CLT its distinctive identity and transformative potential.

To be sure, there are places in the world where CLTs have been effective without adopting every feature of the "classic" CLT. That model is no longer a template, but it remains a touchstone. It is where most people start, when striving to adapt this complex form of tenure to their own situations. It is where most people hope a CLT will lead, when envisioning a better outcome from their arduous, virtuous labors, whether providing affordable housing, rebuilding residential neighborhoods, regularizing tenure in informal settlements, or preserving productive lands and local enterprises at risk of being lost to market pressures.

When land is owned for the common good of a place-based community, present and future; when development is done by an organization that is a creature of that community, rooted in it, accountable to it, and guided by it; when stewardship is deliberate, diligent, and durable . . . justice is more likely to be achieved. And more likely to last. That is the moral impetus and lofty promise of common ground.

Notes

1. Organizationally, the model promoted by the Institute for Community Economics during the 1980s had an open membership and a three-part board, representing the interests of the people who live on the CLT's land, people who live within the CLT's service area, and institutions that served that geography, including government, churches, banks, businesses, and other NGOs. See Institute for Community Economics, *The Community Land Trust Handbook* (Emmaus PA: Rodale Press, 1982).

2. To a certain degree, we sidestepped this definitional debate in our 2020 book, *On Common Ground: International Perspectives on the Community Land Trust*, by featuring organizations that self-identify as a community land trust, even if they do not exhibit every feature of what is known in the USA as the "classic" CLT. Our ecumenical embrace had limits, however. We admitted to the company of CLTs only organizations that were committed to removing land permanently from the stream of commerce, placing it under the ownership or control of a designated community and stewarding that land for the common good.

3. This echoes the earliest description of the CLT: "The community land trust is not primarily concerned with common ownership. Rather, its concern is ownership for the common good, which may or may not be combined with common ownership." International Independence Institute (1972), op cit., page 1. Although the people living on a CLT's land do not hold title to the underlying land, the resale formula used by some CLTs does provide for a modest increase in the homeowner's equity if the land has appreciated in value during the homeowner's tenure.

4. Trusts are established by individuals to control the distribution of their property, either during their lifetimes or after their death. Property is often real estate, but it may also be stocks, bonds, or other income-generating assets. The person who creates the trust is called the "settlor." The person who holds the property for another's behalf is the "trustee." The latter takes title to the property, although under a "revocable trust" the settlor may later reclaim ownership. Proceeds from the trust are distributed by the trustee to a specific list of beneficiaries named by the settlor when the trust was established. Trusts like these bear little resemblance to the way in which nearly all CLTs are organized and operated.

1.

The Once and Future Garden City

Yves Cabannes and Philip Ross

Over 100 years ago, Ebenezer Howard set out on an intellectual journey to define what would make a Garden City. The result, in 1898, was his book *Garden Cities of To-Morrow — A Peaceful Path to Real Reform*. It was written in an age when the memory of the Paris Commune was still fresh, when Marxism was still being formulated, when imperial Europe was at its zenith, and when a young Lenin was still in a reflective mood. It was written in the shadow of the co-operative movement which showed that people were capable of coming together to build their own institutions. In the late 1800s, there were around 27,000 registered mutual societies.

The book led to the founding of Letchworth Garden City, the world's first Garden City. Howard had been reflecting on the industrialisation process that was still underway in Britain at the time. He aimed to bring the best of town and country together in the ideal town. In Howard's vision, the citizen would be King and the ills of the time — landlords, squalor, pollution and poverty — would be tackled and beaten.

Printed word became reality when funding was found to purchase a large parcel of land on which to build this new town. As Letchworth took shape, inspiring architecture was a key component and the layout of the town was planned with simple rules that reflected common sense. For example, factories were placed in the east so the smoke didn't blow over the town. The architects were inspired by the Arts and Crafts Movement and driven by a belief in green spaces, a healthy environment, and a sympathetic layout.[1] These were the watchwords guiding this new utopia.

However, Howard and his supporters knew that there was more to a good community and a vibrant town than a carefully designed site plan and attractive architecture. The social aspects would be of equal importance, with ownership and citizenship the key ingredients. A Garden City was designed to be just and fair for the people who would live there. At its heart was the radical proposition of the common ownership of land. This was

1

Fig. 1.1. Letchworth today, still alive and beautiful. YVES CABANNES

important because the Garden City needed to be more than a well-meaning attempt to build affordable homes. Although Howard may have articulated it differently, the Garden City needed to be sustainable in the longer term. It needed to be economically sustainable in its own right, which is why the capture of rising land values was crucial. Community-owned land was needed if the Garden City was to be socially sustainable and to maintain a balance of affordability as land values rose. The Garden City also needed to be ecologically sustainable in terms of its impact on the environment. Planning played a part here, as did local food production, which was built into the heart of the model. But underlying it all was the notion that the Garden City should own itself.

Letchworth's socialist architects, Barry Parker and Raymond Unwin, were soon helping to design the Hampstead Garden suburb and other areas in the UK, including Welwyn Garden City in England, built on a grander scale than Letchworth. The Garden City Movement quickly crossed the English Channel and inspired Cités Jardins in the Coal Mining Region of Northern France as early as 1905, and new towns around Brussels just after the First World War. Garden Cities appeared around Paris, as well as in Germany, Switzerland, Portugal, and The Netherlands. There were also a number established around Moscow, a result of Howard's book having been translated into Russian as early as 1912, inspiring Russian city planners before and after the 1917 Bolshevik Revolution.

Garden Cities and Garden Neighbourhoods soon expanded beyond the European borders. They appeared in Cairo, Buenos Aires, and Santiago to name a few. Brazil deserves a special mention since Barry Parker, one of the principal planners of Letchworth, advised the City of São Paulo in establishing the Jardim America development between 1917 and 1919. This was the starting point for a significant number of Garden Neighbourhoods and Garden Cities throughout Brazil—more than 45 of them. The concept of Garden Cities also influenced planning in North America. Three Greenbelt towns built during the 1930s — Greendale, Wisconsin; Greenhills, Ohio; and Green-belt, Maryland — are among the most iconic examples.[2]

It is now more than 110 years since the founding of the first Garden City. With all this history and experience of town design, community development, and various applications of the Garden City model, it is time to ask what lessons can be learned. What should the principles of a 21st Century Garden City be? We believe that many of Howard's original instincts were correct, but how can his vision for the Garden City be delivered in a modern setting?

GUIDING PRINCIPLES OF A GARDEN CITY

The place to start is with a declaration that a Garden City is a fair, just, and harmonious community. It should be a place that is economically, socially and ecologically sustainable. It is not restricted to new cities or towns, even to those that were built following traditional Garden City town planning, architectural, or design principles. A Garden City is about community, not merely about architecture and urban design. It is about building a harmonious community, balancing and combining the best of town and country to create a community where the measure of success is ultimately the happiness of the people who live in it.

As described in a "manifesto" we published in 2014, there are twelve principles that we believe underlie a Garden City in the 21st Century.[3] They are inspired by Howard's ideas, by the legacy of Letchworth, and by successful international practice. We declare that any town or city or neighbourhood can be considered a Garden City if it embraces the following principles:

- Residents are citizens.

- The Garden City owns itself.

- The Garden City is energy efficient and carbon neutral.

- The Garden City provides access to land for living and working to all.

- Fair Trade principles are practised.

- Prosperity is shared.

- All citizens are equal, all citizens are different.

- There is fair representation and direct democracy.

- Garden Cities are produced through participatory planning and design methods.

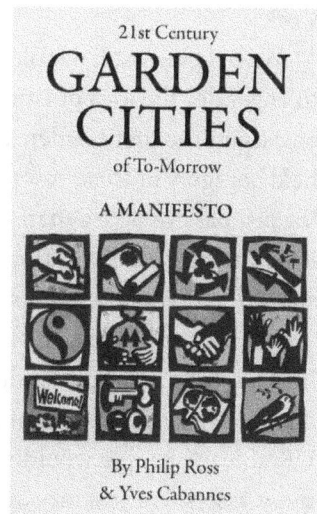

21st Century

GARDEN CITIES

of To-Morrow

A MANIFESTO

By Philip Ross
& Yves Cabannes

Fig. 1.2. Cover of the 2014 "Manifesto." Earlier editions appeared in 2012 and 2013.

- A City of Rights builds and defends the Right to the City.

- Knowledge is held in common, shared and enhanced.

- Wealth and harmony are measured by happiness.

These principles represent multiple doorways into the Garden City. You can enter using any of them, but deny or contradict any one of them and they become exits. Let's concentrate, however, on the principle that is most relevant to community land trusts: "the Garden City owns itself." That doesn't mean that CLTs do not also strive to put the other principles into practice. But land that is owned and managed for the common good is the main intersection between the Garden City and the CLT.

THE GARDEN CITY OWNS ITSELF

The Garden City is ultimately owned by its local community and not by a series of landlords. This ownership and governance is derived from the people who live and work in the city and who are its citizens acting for the common good. If the Garden City is its own landlord, then it is answerable to and controlled by its citizens, ideally as a community land trust managed by democratic structures that make it both inclusive and accountable.

This principle is the most powerful of all because it is a tangible realisation of citizenship. It is about the real and tangible ownership of the Garden City. It is about common and collective forms of tenure of the city and citizen control of the assets within it. Ownership itself isn't enough, however. There must also be participation: active citizens who are capable of holding the landowner to account. Otherwise the Garden City will not work.

We believe that if people who live in a city have a stake in its prosperity, that will help to engender the idea of citizenship. This is what Ebenezer Howard understood when he envisaged the first Garden City. The Garden City was not to be a charity or something held benignly in trust; it was to have common ownership. Nor was it about people holding just passive paper-shares in the city, speculating on its success, but instead participating in it, building it, making it an "oeuvre d'art"— making it a masterpiece, sharing in its success, and shouldering its responsibilities as well.

The owner of the city's landed assets — or the owner of land underlying a neighborhood—isn't a distant landlord, nor is it the local city council or central government. Nominally, the assets might be placed under the control of the "local council," but in the UK at least, people wouldn't have confidence that the council would defend or protect those assets. For instance, many people believe that if the assets in Letchworth had been placed under control of the district council, they would have been sold off piecemeal over the years to fund lower taxes and to gain political favour with voters. Instead, by locking the assets inside of a trust, Letchworth's lands have been kept together for the long-term benefit of the community —"in perpetuity," as community land trust slogans usually say.

Garden Cities are more than just housing, however. Howard's focus — and ours — encompasses the whole town, not just the housing stock. Agriculture, shops, offices, and other commercial spaces, even industry — anything can be located on land that is owned and operated for the common good.

How can this be done? How can people hold the land in common? There are many ways that residents can be their own landlords. This can be done through a co-operative model, a co-operative land bank, or a community land trust.

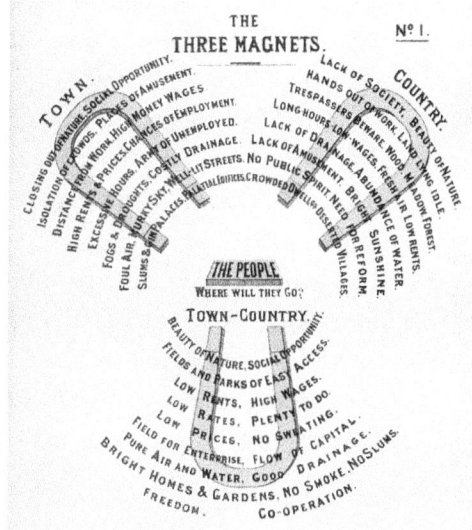

Fig. 1.3. Garden Cities were envisioned to combine the best of town and country, depicted by Howard in his famous image of the "Three Magnets" (right). Letchworth did just that, making land available not only for housing, but for manufacturing (left) and gardening (bottom) as well.
YVES CABANNES

COMMUNITY LAND OWNERSHIP

One of the most successful models of common land ownership is the community land trust (CLT), originated in the United States by Ralph Borsodi and Robert Swann. The prototype for the modern-day community land trust in the USA was formed in 1969 near Albany, Georgia by leaders of the Southern Civil Rights Movement. These CLT pioneers drew upon earlier examples of planned communities on leased land including Howard's Garden Cities, single tax communities in the USA, and Gramdan Villages in India, where wealthy landowners voluntarily gave a percentage of their land, which was then held in trust for lower castes by the entire village.

Basically, a CLT separates the ownership of land from that of any structures that are built on that land. The community land trust retains ownership of the land, whereas houses, commercial buildings, restaurants, etc. sited on that land are sold off, rented out, or owned and managed as cooperatives or for-profit small businesses. We especially like the definition from Diacon, Clarke, and Guimarães on how a CLT works:

> A CLT separates the value of the land from the buildings that stand on it and can be used in a wide range of circumstances to preserve the value of any public and private investment, as well as planning gain and land appreciation for community benefit. Crucially, local residents and businesses are actively involved in planning and delivering affordable local housing, workspace or community facility.[4]

THE UNEARNED INCREMENT

Why bother with this complicated form of ownership? The answer has to do with land values and the fact that they continue to rise. When writing about the revenue of the Garden City and how it might be obtained, Ebenezer Howard said the following:

> Thus, while in some parts of London the rent is equal to £30,000 an acre, £4 an acre is an extremely high rent for agricultural land. This enormous difference of rental value is, of course, almost entirely due to the presence in the one case and the absence in the other of a large population; and, as it cannot be attributed to the action of any particular individuals, it is frequently spoken of as the "unearned increment," i.e. unearned by the landlord, though a more correct term would be "collectively earned increment."
>
> The presence of a considerable population thus giving a greatly additional value to the soil, it is obvious that a migration of population on any considerable scale to any particular area will be certainly attended with a corresponding rise in the value of the land to settled upon, and it is also obvious that such increment of value may, with some foresight and pre-arrangement, become the property of the migrating people.
>
> Such foresight and pre-arrangement, never before exercised in an effective manner,

are displayed conspicuously in the case of Garden City, where the land, as we have seen, is vested in trustees, who hold it in trust (after payment of the debentures) for the whole community, so that the entire increment of value gradually created becomes the property of the city, with the effect that though rents may rise, and even rise considerably, such rise in rent will not become the property of private individuals.[5]

Cost and value of land tend to rise, while wages typically increase at a lesser rate, or remain stagnant. Sometimes this land value rises when the taxpayer invests money in improving the local infrastructure, yet it is property owners (and not tenants or lease-holders) who gain the most benefit. The real winners are those who hold a deed to land.[6]

THE CLT AS A VEHICLE FOR CREATING A GARDEN CITY

Despite the prominence given to community-owned land in Howard's vision of the Garden City, as well as in that vision's early implementation at Letchworth and Welwyn, this guiding principle got diluted over time. In many places that called themselves a Garden City, it disappeared altogether. Sadly it was the architectural and design principles that would be copied and celebrated, as architects tried again and again to build the perfect city or town through bricks and mortar alone. Garden Cities became the acceptable face of town and city planning. Its more radical elements, like the common ownership of land, were often left behind.

Community land trusts are a means of restoring community-owned land to the conception and implementation of the Garden City, as well as a means of revitalizing citizenship, another of our twelve principles for creating a Garden City. CLTs are also a way to remove the biggest obstacle to making Garden Cities a reality today. The Garden City envisioned by Howard had a particularly daunting requirement. A group of trustees had to locate and to acquire 6000 acres of vacant land

> CLTs insist on the essential conjunction between ownership and citizenship.

on which to construct a new town accommodating 32,000 residents. That might have been possible in the early half of 20th Century, as dozens of towns, suburbs, and neighbourhoods were being planned and built, incorporating design features that Parker and Unwin had pioneered at Letchworth. That is less likely to be a real possibility today, especially in settled areas of the Global North.

We would argue, however, that any town or city or neighbourhood can become a Garden City by embracing the twelve principles we identified earlier, including that a "Garden City owns itself." How does that happen, however, if the likelihood of acquiring thousands of acres of vacant land is remote?

Community land trusts provide a partial answer. They are a vehicle for gradually assembling land and putting Garden City principles into practice — now not later. There

Fig. 1.4. Knowledge sharing, a guiding principle of Garden Cities in the 21st Century. Students visiting Letchworth on a rainy day in 2012. YVES CABANNES

is no reason to wait until thousands of acres are purchased. And land doesn't have to be vacant. Even land with buildings already on it can be brought into a CLT, allowing existing neighbourhoods to be transformed over time into something resembling a Garden City. As John Emmeus Davis wrote in the Postscript to our 2014 Manifesto:

> The promise of the CLT was that Garden City principles could be put into practice right away. Something resembling a Garden City could be created incrementally. It could start small and steadily expand. It could construct new buildings or be woven as a bright thread of rehabilitation and renewal into the gray fabric of a built environment already in place.[7]

Not only do community land trusts allow Garden City activists to get started right away. CLTs also insist on the essential conjunction between ownership and citizenship, as do we. While we extol the virtues of community-owned land, this form of ownership can only be effective if it is accountable. It is by being accountable to the community it serves that a CLT can share its prosperity fairly. Yet this accountability only works if residents are empowered enough to realize that individually and collectively they have the power to question, to scrutinize, and to hold to account those who are operating the CLT.

A community land trust is, by its very nature, accountable to the people who inhabit and surround its lands. It is of the upmost importance, therefore, that the governance and management of the CLT be fair and equitable; otherwise, it can quite easily move from being a socially engaged organization to becoming, at best, a paternalistic one; or become, at worst, a neo-feudal one that exercises control, but is not accountable to its community. A CLT without democratic governance and scrutiny could become the worst of all landlords. A CLT that is dominated by a small group has failed; it is no longer the owner of land of the people, by the people, and for the people.

A community land trust that is economically aware and empowered, one that is socially responsible and driven by those principles, and one that is committed to ecologically sustainable practices is a settlement that is truly ready to pick up the torch for Garden Cities in the 21st Century.

For Howard, it may have been a leap of faith to create a Garden City, but today we know that all the principles of the Garden City have been proven in practice. They have been implemented in settlements across the globe. Individually, each makes a positive impact. But the more of them that we can establish and connect, the greater their impact will be.

The Garden City isn't simply a utopian or idealist vision, but a practical one. It works. It can create a community that is socially, economically and ecologically sustainable. There may be different reasons for choosing a model based on these principles, but at the top of the list is the realization that it will deliver a successful and sustainable community for the long term. To those considering adopting such a model, take courage; you do not stand alone. History, common sense, and a whole movement is ready to stand with you.

Notes

1. The Arts and Crafts Movement began in Britain around 1880 and quickly spread to America, Europe, and Japan. Inspired by the ideas of John Ruskin and William Morris, it advocated a revival of traditional handicrafts, a return to a simpler way of life, and an improvement in the design of ordinary domestic objects.

2. Despite its swift expansion, the worldwide Garden Cities movement became disarrayed with the emergence of the modernist movement and the Athens Charter, signed in the mid-1930s. See: Y. Cabannes and P. Ross, "Food Planning in Garden Cities: The Letchworth Legacy," RUAF Working Papers (Leyden: RUAF Foundation International Network of Resource Centres on Urban Agriculture and Food Security, 2018).

3. Philip Ross and Yves Cabannes, *21st Century Garden Cities of To-Morrow: A Manifesto* (2014).

4. D. Diacon, R. Clarke, and S. Guimarães, S. (eds), *Redefining the Commons: Locking in Value through Community Land Trusts,* Joseph Rowntree Foundation (Coalville: Building and Social Housing Foundation, 2005).

5. Ebenezer Howard, *Garden Cities of To-Morrow* (Available at: *http://www.sacred-texts.com/utopia/gcot/gcot04.htm*).

6. In Letchworth, for example, it is the Trust that owns the land and captures the land's rising value. In 2017, the Trust's tangible assets, made up mostly of lands underlying Letchworth, were reported to have a net asset value of £146 million — which was £12 million more than in 2016 (LGC Heritage Foundation, 2018).

7. J.E. Davis, "A Community Land Trust Perspective on Building the Next Generation of Garden Cities." Pp. 187–197 in Philip Ross and Yves Cabannes, op. cit.

2.

Common Ground
Community-Owned Land as a Platform for
Equitable and Sustainable Development[1]

John Emmeus Davis

Land, labor, and capital have long been considered the primary factors of production, regardless of whether one is planning for the fabrication of durable goods in an industrial plant or for the revitalization of dilapidated homes in a residential neighborhood. Every analysis of a project's feasibility begins here. Much creative thought is devoted to these essential inputs, weighing how best to tweak their design, to reduce their cost, and to increase their effectiveness. Creativity of this sort is especially important in community development, where the production of goods and services for people of limited means must be heavily subsidized out of public coffers and private contributions. Every dollar must be inventively stretched and cleverly invested for maximum effect.

Land has been the glaring exception to this predilection for innovation. Experimentation has been the norm in community development when it comes to finding new ways to improve infrastructure, to incubate enterprises, to finance homeownership, or to train low-skilled workers. Far less ingenuity has gone into designing new ways of owning, controlling, and utilizing land to make distressed places more livable or to make prosperous places more inclusive.

This pattern has persisted despite the presence of an innovative model of community-led development on community-owned land that has spread steadily across the United States and is now becoming rooted in other countries as well. Known as the community land trust (CLT), this unconventional approach to place-based development has three distinguishing features: (1) a private, nonprofit organization, acting on behalf of a geographically defined community, acquires and retains scattered parcels of land that are put to a variety of uses through long-term ground leasing; (2) residential or nonresidential buildings located on these leaseholds are sold off to individual owners — families, cooperatives, farmers, small businesses, etc. — whose ownership interest is encumbered by long-lasting affordability controls over each building's use and resale; and (3) the non-profit landowner is guided in the development and stewardship of lands and buildings under its care by people who use its land, occupy its housing, or reside within the surrounding community.

A shorthand description of this strategy, pursued by CLTs and other nongovernmental organizations operating in a similar fashion, is *community-led development of permanently affordable housing (and other assets) on community-owned land.* Or, shorter still, *common ground.*

Any sort of building can be raised on a foundation of community-owned land, although CLTs have devoted most of their resources to date to the production and preservation of housing. On leased land, CLTs have developed many types and tenures of renter-occupied and owner-occupied housing, all priced within the financial reach of persons of limited means. The particular forte of community land trusts is not development, however, but *stewardship*: taking care of this housing long after it is created. CLTs have been effective in preventing the disappearance of affordability when real estate markets are hot and have been equally effective in preventing the erosion of owner equity, the neglect of necessary repairs, and the loss of homes to foreclosure when markets turn cold.

Despite the documented success of CLTs in making such "counter-cyclical stewardship" a reality, many nonprofit organizations in the United States have been slow to incorporate common ground into their programs.[2] The simplest explanation for their hesitancy is that doing development on community-owned land is hard work, especially when a community's residents are given a say in deciding how land should be used and developed. Most nonprofit housing developers choose an easier path. They sell off local lands. They shut out local voices. They roll out affordably priced housing that looks familiar to public funders and private lenders, while minimizing their own responsibility for preserving the affordability, quality, and security of those homes after they are built.

This essay argues that common ground is worth the extra effort. It is a strategy for redistribution, putting property and power into the hands of people deprived of both. It is also a bulwark against loss, protecting hard-won gains in ownership and empowerment from leaking away over time. For *impoverished* neighborhoods needing revitalization, CLTs allow investment to occur and development to proceed without the wholesale displacement of lower-income households, low-profit enterprises, and beloved spaces that populated an area before it began to improve. For *prosperous* neighborhoods lacking economic and racial diversity, CLTs allow housing to be produced for lower-income people that will remain affordable forever. On the platform of common ground, equitable development and sustainable development become two sides of the same coin. Places are made more just. Justice is made to last.

I. REDISTRIBUTION:
THE PURSUIT OF EQUITABLE DEVELOPMENT

Every investigation into whether place-based development is *equitable* begins with a question that city planners ask less frequently than they should: *Cui bono,* who benefits? Equally relevant is the converse: Who's harmed? When new investment is brought into a neighborhood, when new housing is built, when social conditions improve and land values rise, the lion's share of the benefits will go either to people in need or to people who already possess an abundance of property and power. Similarly, the burdens of development will either be apportioned fairly or fall disproportionately upon the shoulders of people who are least able to bear them.

> Common ground tips the scales in favor of people who have been excluded from the benefits of land-based wealth and who have lacked the power to shape development.

Strategies and outcomes of place-based development are always to be found somewhere along the contested continuum between these poles. Either they tilt toward *redistribution,* challenging the existing landscape of inequality, or they tilt toward *reinforcement,* etching patterns of privilege more deeply into the social structure of place. Common ground does the former. It tips the scales in favor of people who have been excluded from the benefits of land-based wealth and who have lacked the power to shape development within their own neighborhoods, be those places urban, suburban, or rural.

A. Street Level Land Reform:
The Economic Case for Common Ground

The community land trust is a hybrid of three strategies used around the world to redistribute landed resources to achieve a more equitable allocation of income and wealth. In their commitment to community-owned land, CLTs are part of a *collective tradition* of land reform in which private estates or public lands are transferred intact to collectives, cooperatives, or village trusts.[3] In their commitment to expanding individual access to lands and buildings, CLTs are inheritors of a *distributionist tradition* in which concentrated landholdings are broken into smaller homesteads and put into the hands of families, farmers, and entrepreneurs. In its commitment to the fair allocation of appreciating real estate values, CLTs are part of a long tradition of *value recapture* that can be traced from the "social increment" of John Stuart Mill, through the Single Tax crusade of Henry George, to the Garden Cities of Ebenezer Howard.[4]

CLTs are unique not only in combining these three traditions of land reform, but in doing so at a different *level* than attempted in the past. Most land reform schemes have been targeted to an entire country. By contrast, community land trusts are tailored to fit the geography and circumstances of place-based communities as small as a single neighborhood, city, or county. Even when a CLT carves out a much larger geography, the economic benefits of common ground are realized at the micro-level of neighborhood and household.

Common ground is a versatile foundation on which any type of building can be constructed and on which any use of land can be secured. Although most CLT activity has centered on expanding access to affordable housing, the lands owned by CLTs have also been used in the development of community centers, day care centers, office space for other NGOs, and commercial buildings for neighborhood retail. Community-owned land has been leased out for community gardens, greenhouses, and commercial farming. In more rural areas, CLTs have been used to preserve access to productive lands for small farmers.

Although some CLTs are heavily involved in developing rental housing, home-ownership has been the priority of most community land trusts in the United States. By boosting lower-income people into homeownership, either in houses, townhouses, condominiums, or cooperatives, CLTs put these households on a path toward stabilizing their finances and, over time, toward increasing their personal wealth.

CLTs are hardly alone in using public subsidies and private donations to make home-ownership more widely available. There are two significant advantages, however, that community-owned land and long-term ground leasing bring to the whole business of building economic prosperity for low-income people when helping them to buy a home.

First, common ground is an effective shield against financial shocks that can strip low-income people of the prosperity they thought was theirs when purchasing a home. A painful lesson of the Great Recession was that personal wealth, when embedded in residential real estate, is less secure than commonly assumed. Homeowners only build wealth if they can hang onto their homes, which many could not when the Recession hit and the mortgage market collapsed. Between 2007 and 2012, 12.5 million market-rate, owner-occupied homes went into foreclosure in the United States. Communities of color bore the brunt of it, due in large measure to the higher incidence of homes that had been mortgaged using high-priced, variable-rate subprime loans.[5]

The owners of resale-restricted homes developed by CLTs fared much better, experiencing rates of default and foreclosure during the worst of the Great Recession that were a tenth of the rate experienced by the owners of market-rate homes.[6] What the former had that the latter did not was a partner that stood protectively between them and their lenders. At the front end of the lending process, the CLT was by their side, reviewing and approving proposed mortgages and preventing predatory lending. Later on, the CLT was prepared to act on their behalf, should the owners of resale-restricted homes get behind in their payments, intervening to halt foreclosure and to prevent the loss of household wealth. The CLT's stewardship regime was not only effective in preserving affordability for the *next* generation of homebuyers, therefore; it also proved effective in preserving the equity invested and earned by the *current* generation of homeowners.

Community land trusts have also shown themselves to be unusually effective at capturing and distributing land-based wealth inter-generationally. They do so by preventing the removal of public and private subsidies invested in the privately-owned housing on their lands. Subsidies that are retained in CLT homes (along with much of a home's appreciation) reduce the price for subsequent buyers, in effect sharing land-based wealth between one generation of homeowners and another. This feat of redistribution, achieved through a pricing formula and preemptive option embedded in the ground lease, puts the CLT squarely within the land reform tradition of value recapture pioneered by Henry George and Ebenezer Howard, while adding a street-level focus contemplated by neither.

B. Empowerment of Community:
The Political Case for Common Ground

A particular strength of community-owned land is the opportunity provided to a place-based community to impose its will on *what* is developed and *how* development is done, making collective decisions about the common good. As Harry Smith has said about the CLT created by the Dudley Street Neighborhood Initiative in Boston, "The land trust doesn't exist just to acquire and manage land. It's really about engaging community to decide together what they want on their land."[7]

Land that is *community-owned* provides a foundation for development that is *community-led*. This is more than simply opening up a developer's planning process to community participation, inviting residents to voice opinions about the kind of improvements needed to make their neighborhood nicer, safer, or more affordable. A nonprofit organization that owns and manages leaseholds has a head start on creating a place-based constituency that is capable of defending and advancing the interests of everyone who calls that neighborhood their home.

1. Sharing Power

Among the myriad NGOs doing community development in the United States, there has been a notable decline in the number that incorporate participatory strategies and structures into their organizations and operations. Too many have drifted away from what used to be an article of faith among nonprofits dedicated to housing low-income people or to revitalizing low-income neighborhoods; namely, a core belief that the beneficiaries of an organization's projects and services should have a voice in planning those activities and in guiding and governing the organization that carries them out.

A philosophical commitment to democratic governance may help to arrest that slide, although that is hardly unique to CLTs. What *is* unique to a CLT is the practical necessity of anticipating and managing the risk of leaseholder discontent. Landowner-leaseholder relations are not always smooth. Indeed, they can become downright bumpy, an ever-present possibility in the dual-ownership intricacies and intimacies of ground leasing. A desire to reduce the severity of these clashes and to protect its own reputation in the larger community can be strong incentives for a nonprofit landowner to create a structure and culture for leaseholder engagement. The easiest way for a nonprofit organization to ensure that its beneficiaries are cheerleaders rather than critics is to make them partners in guiding and governing the organization itself.

Cost is a factor in this calculation. The least expensive stewardship regime is one in which compliance is routine and enforcement is unnecessary, one in which the occupants of price-restricted buildings police themselves, voluntarily abiding by the contractual conditions that encumber their homes. Compliance with these restrictions is more likely when the people whose homes are encumbered are given a voice in directing the activities of the organization that is managing the land beneath their feet and overseeing the buildings in which they live.

2. Building Power

A nonprofit that is holding land on behalf of a place-based community and doing ground leasing cannot confine its activities to being a developer; it must be an educator and organizer as well. That is not only because its leaseholders may sometimes insist on their "landlord" entering the fray on their behalf, but also because the difficulties that accompany this unconventional form of tenure make it necessary for a nonprofit lessor to build awareness and acceptance at the same time it is building housing. The very things that make ground leasing harder to implement and to manage tend to force any nonprofit doing ground leasing to behave (at times) like a community organizer and to use (on occasion) whatever power it has accumulated to defend the interests of its leaseholders, its community, and itself.

> Land that is community-owned provides a foundation for development that is community-led.

Building power for a CLT begins with the "captive audience" of the organization's own leaseholders. As Jesse Myerson has observed, "Land removed from the private market, decommodified and placed under the ownership and management of the people who live there, is land that creates and renews its own political constituency."[8] This constituency is helped to grow by the versatility of ground leasing, where anything can be developed on community-owned land. When a nonprofit organization takes full advantage of this versatility, shopkeepers, service providers, and community gardeners are added to the ranks of residential leaseholders, broadening the base of a CLT's support.

C. Development with Justice:
The Preservationist Case for Common Ground

Most place-based development is aimed at aggressively rebuilding impoverished localities in which an absence of investment has caused conditions inimical to surviving and thriving for all residents. But place-based development may also be aimed at *prosperous* localities, where an abundance of investment (combined, perhaps, with a pernicious dose of discriminatory zoning) has elevated land values and left little room for housing that is affordable, effectively excluding the poor and people of color. Equitable development is not only about lifting up the worst places; it is also about opening up the best places.

In both situations, the special dilemma for practitioners committed to producing equitable outcomes is how to protect redistributive gains that are achieved in the present against their steady erosion by market forces in the future; even more, how to avoid inadvertently accelerating that process by a practitioner's own success in turning a neighborhood around. The preservationist case for common ground addresses this dilemma head-on, arguing that common ground can provide a foundation for equitable development *and* sustainable development, enabling the implementation of both.

1. Do No Harm

Public agencies, private foundations, and community development organizations of every stripe too rarely *plan for success* when endeavoring to improve distressed neighborhoods. They seem unable to imagine a day when their own efforts might cause property values to rise and market pressures to mount, threatening the wellbeing of the disadvantaged population they set out to help. Focused so intently on doing something good for places urgently in need, these well-meaning interventionists provide no protection against the possibility of something bad happening down the road.

Planning for success when *equitable* development is the goal begins by honestly acknowledging the pain that place-based development often inflicts on economically precarious people and accepting responsibility for doing something to prevent it. By that light, any funder or practitioner who intervenes in a low-income neighborhood with the intention of bettering the lives of those residing there should approach such places with a caution and humility akin to that embodied in the Hippocratic Oath: "Take care that they suffer no hurt or damage."

One of the surest ways of "taking care" is for a community to "Take a Stand, Own the Land," as the organizing slogan of the Dudley Street Neighborhood Initiative (DSNI) once put it. In the 1970s, residents of the Boston neighborhood of Roxbury welcomed the prospect that transit-oriented development might attract investment into an area that had experienced decades of redlining, abandonment, and arson for profit. But they also worried that rising rents and prices might follow in its wake, displacing families with limited incomes. The solution championed by DSNI was to begin acquiring a significant percentage of the neighborhood's land *before* it was caught up in market forces that the government's investment in infrastructure would unleash. A community land trust subsidiary named Dudley Neighbors Inc. (DNI) was established by DSNI in 1988 to hold that land, while also preserving the affordability of any rental housing, cooperative housing, and owner-occupied houses, duplexes, and triplexes constructed on its land.[9]

A similar strategy has been pursued in the Tenderloin neighborhood of San Francisco, where a long-standing partnership between municipal agencies and nonprofit providers of affordable housing has resulted in a steady stream of land being moved into social ownership over the span of many years:

> Starting in the 1970s and continuing uninterrupted over the decades since, Tenderloin activists, working with city government and a set of strong nonprofit partners, bought or otherwise obtained control over a significant share of the area's real estate. . . . It's a 'win-win' strategy that could be dismissed as wishful thinking in any other contested neighborhood. But in the Tenderloin, community control of land makes it possible for community leaders to risk improving the neighborhood without worrying that new investment will push out all the low income people. . . . In fact, this strategy of steady land acquisition and permanent affordability controls is probably the only approach to combating gentrification that can actually win.[10]

Community-owned land cannot prevent market forces from buffeting a neighborhood, any more than an umbrella can stop the rain. It cannot prevent affluent people from moving into a low-income area that is newly attractive to homebuyers and entrepreneurs who, sensing a change in the area's fortunes, are now willing to settle their families or businesses there. What community-owned land *can* do is to keep the poor from getting drowned in the deluge. It is a bulwark against displacement, protecting clusters of affordably priced housing that funders and practitioners have worked so hard to create; preventing endangered islands of security and opportunity from being washed away.

Affordable housing is not the only "lower" land use that is threatened when neighborhoods improve. The same is true for many nonresidential land uses that serve and employ people of modest means. Here, too, common ground can be a bulwark against displacement. A community-based organization that holds land under a variety of buildings and leases out land for a variety of purposes can prevent the loss of small manufacturers, retail establishments, artist spaces, community facilities, and open lands that are put under pressure whenever real estate values rapidly rise. It can also preserve cooperatively owned enterprises that may be tempted to "demutualize" when the enterprise thrives.[11]

Especially vulnerable in neighborhoods undergoing rapid improvement are the sites that Ray Oldenburg has called "third places."[12] These are informal, celebratory spaces in which neighboring occurs and community happens. Often, the most endangered of these spaces in neighborhoods having large concentrations of lower-income people are community gardens. When a neighborhood is economically depressed, the supply of land for community gardens is often cheap and plentiful. When the neighborhood rebounds and land values rise, sometimes as a result of public investment or as a result of residents cleaning up vacant lots and planting verdant gardens, third spaces devoted to urban agriculture are among the first to go.[13]

> In places where the economic tide has turned, common ground can bend the arc of prosperity toward justice.

In sum, common ground can serve as a durable protection for people, uses, and spaces that were tenaciously there long before a disadvantaged place began to improve. It can help to ensure that the *benefits* of development do not accrue primarily to the few who had the foresight and fortune to buy up a neighborhood's real estate when prices were depressed. It can help to ensure that the *burdens* of development do not fall disproportionately on individuals who are the least able to bear them. In places where the economic tide has turned, often as a direct or indirect result of the intervention of public funders, private foundations, and nonprofit developers, common ground can bend the arc of prosperity toward justice.

2. Make It Last

Conditions of surviving and thriving for persons of limited means are not only lacking in places of poverty, they are also lacking in many places of prosperity. The usual culprit in the latter is the scarcity of affordable housing. Low-income people may work in affluent neighborhoods, suburbs, and towns. They may shop there. But they often cannot live there, excluded by rents and prices far beyond their reach.[14]

Opening up privileged enclaves from which low-income families and people of color are regularly barred has been as much a focus of community land trusts in the United States as improving distressed neighborhoods in which underprivileged populations are concentrated. At present, there are even more CLTs working in areas where housing prices are robust than in places where housing prices are depressed. Despite the differences between strong-market cities and weak-market cities, there is often a similar lack of attention that is paid by policymakers to protecting whatever success they have had in improving conditions for people of limited means. Similar, too, is the preservationist role that CLTs have been asked to play.

Most affordably priced homes produced in affluent areas would not exist without the investment of public dollars from a federal, state, or city agency, without the imposition of municipal mandates like inclusionary zoning, or without the beneficence of density bonuses, parking waivers, tax abatements, land donations, infrastructure extensions, and other incentives. Governmental intervention and governmental largess are essential to making newly constructed housing "affordable," allowing homes to rent or to sell for below-market prices that are within the financial reach of people on the lower half of the income ladder.

In too many places, however, this heavily subsidized affordability is not designed to last very long. Restrictions (if any) are imposed on rents and resales that are allowed to lapse after five, fifteen, or thirty years. Prices may then rapidly rise to meet the market. Public subsidies get stuffed into private pockets. Low-income people get displaced. This programmed loss of publicly assisted, privately owned housing has been a dominant feature of most housing policy in the United States, at all levels of government, for decades.[15]

Calm acceptance of the planned attrition of subsidized housing was shaken by the affordability crisis of the 1980s and 1990s and by the foreclosure crisis of the Great Recession in 2007–2009. These disruptions caused a grudging shift in the tectonic plates of American housing policy. At the municipal level, in particular, increased attention began to be paid to preventing the loss of publicly subsidized housing, whether to market pricing, deferred maintenance, or foreclosure.[16] That was especially true in stronger markets where regulatory measures like inclusionary zoning were being used to bring this housing into being. The disappointing performance of many of the earliest cities that adopted inclusionary housing programs, where thousands of affordably priced homes were lost to the market because of short-term affordability controls, provided a corrective lesson for later adopters. Municipal officials began paying closer attention to preserving the affordability of inclusionary housing for a much longer period of time.[17] Stewardship rose higher on the public agenda.

That has created an opportunity for CLTs to show they can do what conventional tenures and programs do not, since stewardship is what community land trusts do best. They stay in the picture long after affordably priced housing has been produced, making sure that it lasts. CLTs, in this regard, are the ultimate preservationists: acting to ensure the lasting affordability and continuing upkeep of privately owned homes, while helping to ensure the ongoing success of the homeowners or renters who occupy them. As Connie Chavez, the former executive director of the Sawmill Community Land Trust in Albuquerque, New Mexico was fond of saying, "We are the developer that doesn't go away."

II. RESILIENCY:
THE PURSUIT OF SUSTAINABLE DEVELOPMENT

Community land trusts are not the only way to preserve the affordable housing that a local government or a private charity has helped to create. Other models and mechanisms are often tapped to play this stewardship role by government officials and housing professionals, who consider them equivalent to the CLT. From their perspective, it "doesn't matter" which method is used as long as subsidies are retained, affordability is perpetuated, and homeowners (and renters) are helped to hang onto their homes.[18]

The assumption of equivalency may actually be true, as long as nothing goes wrong. But stability can be hard to come by. The fortunes of low-income people, low-income neighborhoods, and the nonprofit organizations that serve them are constantly in flux and unavoidably precarious. Among the private developers of subsidized housing, for example, there may be shenanigans in trying to bypass affordability and eligibility restrictions that encumber their properties. Among the owners of resale-restricted homes, there may be delays in doing repairs or delinquencies in paying their mortgages. Among

> Place-based development is equitable only if it can be sustained. It is worth sustaining only if it is equitable.

organizations charged with stewardship, there may be lapses in intervening when housing is at risk. There may be flaws in the organizations themselves, moreover, leading to a failure to thrive — or a failure to fulfill their stewardship responsibilities.

If affordable housing is to be preserved, the contractual and organizational system put in place to make it last must be able to withstand such challenges. It must be able to cope with occasions when people and organizations do not behave as they should. It must not only plan for success; it must also plan for failure. In a word, that system of stewardship must be *resilient*.

Just as equitable development revolves around the question of "who benefits," sustainable development hinges on the question of "how long" — with *forever* being the end to which practitioners aspire. These are overlapping concerns: making it fair and making it last go hand in hand. Place-based development is equitable only if it can be sustained. It is *worth* sustaining only if it is equitable.

Sustainability, for purposes of the present discussion, is couched narrowly in terms of preserving affordable housing and other facilities, spaces, and activities made available for people of limited means, rather than in terms of conserving the natural resources of a limited planet — the more familiar meaning of "sustainable development."[19] Narrowing the discussion further still, our focus is on the preservation of resale-restricted, owner-occupied homes on land belonging to a CLT. This provides something of a test case, showing how the model can perform in challenging circumstances. If the affordability, quality, and security of *owner-occupied* homes are likely to last when homes are sited on a CLT's land, then *other* types and tenures of housing should be sustainable as well.

My argument is this: When it comes to sustainability, preserving affordably priced homeownership in the face of market pressures and changing conditions, common ground is not "equivalent" to other models and mechanisms. It is better. There are advantages to be found in the long-term leasing of community-owned land that cannot be matched by other approaches to stewardship. These advantages allow a CLT to continue doing good even when things go bad.

A. Dependable Intervention:
The Operational Case for Common Ground

Operationally, CLTs are in a league of their own when assigned responsibility for watching over homes entrusted into their care. By owning the land beneath resale-restricted housing, CLTs are more likely to know when their homeowners are having problems. CLTs are more likely to prevail in negotiations with private lenders to prevent these problems from leading to the loss of lands and buildings from the organization's portfolio. CLTs are more likely to intervene when problems arise.

1. Intelligence

One of the keys to effective stewardship is learning about difficulties long before they become too serious to solve and too costly to fix. A particular advantage of community-owned land is that ground leasing contains a formal and informal "early warning system" that other programs for boosting low-income households into homeownership do not.

The *formal* components of this system are: (1) the collection of ground lease fees from homeowners; and (2) the notification from lenders of any mortgage delinquencies. The revenues raised from lease fees are useful in covering a portion of the steward's operating costs, but they serve another function as well. They give the CLT's staff a regular glimpse into how the organization's leaseholders are faring. The first thing the owners of buildings on leased land tend to stop paying, when experiencing financial distress, are the lease fees owed to the benevolent owner of the land beneath their feet. A pattern of late fee payments or mounting arrearages is usually an indication of more serious problems, alerting a CLT of the need to intervene.

Most CLTs selling homes on leased land have a second tripwire built into their system. They become a party to the mortgages on houses or condominiums. Lenders agree to notify the landowner if any homeowners become seriously delinquent in their payments. A lender may do the same when receiving an application to refinance a home on leased land. Such notifications alert the CLT to changes in a leaseholder's financial circumstances that may jeopardize the homeowner's ability to hang onto his or her home.

The *informal* components of a lessor's early warning system are: (1) the continuing relationship between lessor and lessee; and (2) the continuing visibility of the landowner in the eyes of neighbors and city officials. The very structure of ground leasing requires the landowner and homeowners to stay in touch and, to some degree, to get along. If this relationship is a good one, homeowners are more likely to volunteer information about disruptions in their financial situations, giving the CLT an opportunity to help. This marriage of convenience is forged early in the process of preparing prospective homebuyers for life on the steward's land. "During every community land trust homebuyer education class," says Devika Goetschius, director of the CLT in Petaluma, California, "I've looked each person in the eye and told them, 'When your financial circumstances change — good or bad — you call me.'" With admirable regularity, they do.[20]

Admittedly, any organization that serves as the steward for resale-restricted, owner-occupied housing can establish a trusting relationship with those who are buying the organization's homes. My argument is that such a bond is more likely to exist in programs where the steward owns the underlying land. That is partly a consequence of the landowner and homeowner being materially and psychologically tied together, but it is also a function of the CLT being constantly reminded of this relationship by parties looking on from outside. Neighbors are likely to complain to the landowner when homes are not kept in good repair or when lots become cluttered with junk cars. City officials are likely to notify the landowner when there are violations of building or zoning codes, or when homeowners fail to pay special assessments or property taxes. Such pesky calls provide a CLT's staff with valuable on-the-ground intelligence of any looming problems in the CLT's portfolio of resale-restricted housing.

2. Leverage

Owning the underlying land gives a CLT a wider range of options in dealing with a homeowner who is not complying with provisions in her ground lease; for example, not occupying the home as her primary residence or not keeping the home in good repair. The landowner's ultimate leverage in compelling compliance is the threat of eviction from the leasehold, but ground leases also contain a graduated series of less-drastic warnings, penalties, arbitration, and opportunities for injunctive relief. Nearly all violations are corrected long before reaching the dire straits of a CLT acting to remove a homeowner from the land.

Equally important, ownership of the underlying land gives a community land trust greater leverage in negotiating with a private lender or public funder who holds a mortgage on a troubled home. What is mortgaged in most ground leasing programs — and what a lender is allowed to seize if a loan goes bad — is the building, *not* the land. This strengthens the CLT's hand, multiplying the possibilities for dealing with mortgage defaults and foreclosures. The lender may enlist the CLT's cooperation in negotiating a workout with the homeowner, keeping the mortgage in place while putting the homeowner on a schedule to resolve the delinquency. Or the CLT may accept a deed-in-lieu-of-foreclosure from the homeowner. Or the CLT may decide to buy back the house from the lender, following foreclosure.

In short, even when a home (or other building) slides toward foreclosure, and even should a foreclosure actually occur, the community land trust stays stubbornly in the picture.[21] The landowner's presence, interests, and powers cannot be ignored.

3. Intervention

Any NGO that has agreed to serve as the long-term steward of resale-restricted housing is likely to reserve the right to intervene in order to preserve the homeownership opportunities it has worked so hard to create, regardless of whether such authority is granted through a ground lease, a deed covenant, or some other mechanism. But having the *right* to intervene is not the same as having the *will* to do so. In this regard, the long-term leasing of community-owned land comes out ahead.

It is not that the people who run CLTs are more virtuous or energetic than the leaders of other NGOs; rather, their *incentive* to intervene is greater when problems arise. When the homes for which the steward is responsible are located on land that the steward owns, it is harder for that organization to ignore its stewardship responsibilities. To put it bluntly, the steward is "stuck." Those buildings that are not being maintained? They are

> Stewardship is more certain when the organization assigned
> responsibility for stewardship is not only vigilant but vested,
> ensnarled in a benevolent web of its own making.

on the steward's land. Those homes with taxes or mortgages in arrears? They are on the steward's land. And everybody knows it, especially any governmental agencies that may have granted or loaned money to the CLT to develop that housing.

In the face of the many *dis*incentives to intervention, including the time required, the money involved, and the risk of antagonizing homeowners who would rather be left alone, stewards using mechanisms other than a ground lease are more likely to decide that the cost is simply too high to go to the extra trouble of rescuing a distressed property. Owning the land tends to nudge this calculation in the opposite direction, creating an incentive to act that outweighs the disinclination to do so. Ground leasing, in this regard, is what behavioral economists call a *commitment device.*[22] It locks a CLT into living up to its own promises, raising the reputational cost of not intervening to protect the buildings upon its land. Stewardship is more certain when the organization assigned responsibility for stewardship is not only vigilant but vested, ensnarled in a benevolent web of its own making, compelled to do the right thing even when tempted to look the other way.

B. Graceful Failure:
The Organizational Case for Common Ground

An under-appreciated function of common ground is that it tends to make organizational failure less likely and, should a CLT begin to founder, to render its distress or demise less disastrous. Common ground builds greater resiliency into a stewardship regime.

It might seem self-defeating to mention failure while extolling the virtues of community-owned land and long-term ground leasing, but the emphasis here is on what is known as "graceful failure." This is a fault-tolerant principle lifted from the world of engineering and computer programming, where complex systems are designed to continue operating properly even when there is a failure in one of the components. Engineers do not set themselves the impossible goal of building a transportation network, an electrical grid, or a computer program that will never fail. They strive, instead, to create systems that are robust and resilient. Such a system, when subjected to extreme conditions, may bend, but it does not break. Should it crash, it does so with enough warning and backup so as to protect its most valuable components.

Graceful failure is designed into a housing delivery system whenever stewardship is added as a backup for low-cost homes and low-income households assisted with public or private dollars. A stewardship regime makes failure less likely. It also helps to ensure that when failures do occur, which cannot be entirely avoided when dealing with economically vulnerable people, structurally vulnerable assets, and a hopelessly convoluted system for regulating, financing, and subsidizing affordable housing, these failures will not be catastrophic. When stewardship accompanies the deal, homes are more likely to last.

Earlier, it was argued that the *operational* effectiveness of a stewardship regime is enhanced by a steward's ownership of the land beneath residential buildings for which it is responsible. But what of the *organizational* effectiveness of the steward itself? If it is true that some organization must stay watchfully in the picture for many years for affordability, quality, and security to be preserved, then stewardship must necessarily depend on the viability of that organization. It must have the capacity to do the job and the ability to survive. The steward, too, must be designed to last.

One of the best ways to ensure that a CLT will be around for the long haul is to build a diverse portfolio of revenue-generating assets, thereby reducing the organization's dependency on outside funders. Ground leasing, in this regard, can contribute significantly to a steward's bottom line, depending on the magnitude of the organization's holdings. Ground lease fees collected from the owners of buildings on the steward's land can be used to cover a growing portion of the landowner's operating costs, especially those incurred in meeting its stewardship responsibilities. Furthermore, when that portfolio includes multi-unit rental housing on leased land, and perhaps commercial buildings as well, the operational revenue from lease fees can become substantial.

But many CLT's will never develop a sizable and diverse portfolio. Smaller CLTs will sometimes (not always) find it harder to survive. Even CLTs with substantial portfolios may be put in jeopardy by a failed project or by a loss in governmental support, caused by a sudden change in the political winds. What matters the most in these situations, whenever a CLT finds itself on shaky ground, is saving the affordable housing into which low-income people have poured their savings and dreams. In a time of crisis, a nonprofit landowner with a charitable mission must think first of the wellbeing of the homeowners (and renters) who live on its land. Its primary obligation is to them. The governing board of a shaky CLT must do whatever is necessary to protect its leaseholders, including perhaps the prudent decision to lease out some of its land for a "higher" use than housing — or even the painful decision to sell some of its land.

The board may be led in more extreme cases of organizational distress to look for a suitor; that is, another nonprofit organization that is willing to absorb the CLT through a corporate merger or one that is willing to accept the CLT's assets upon the latter's dissolution. A steward with land on its books, along with a guaranteed stream of revenue from future lease fees, brings a lucrative dowry to the search for a partner or successor. This can increase the odds of attracting and negotiating an attractive organizational match that will protect the homes on the CLT's land and perpetuate the stewardship regime surrounding them.

The key point, in these cases, is not only that landownership and ground leasing give the board of a faltering organization more options, but also more motivation to pursue them. Similar to a CLT's commitment to oversight and intervention, a lessor and its lessees are married to one another in a mixed-ownership arrangement that is not easy to unwind. The difficulty of doing so can be a good thing in a time of crisis, forcing everyone to slow down, dig in, and work harder to solve the organization's problems. When there is more at stake, as there is when low-income households live on land that is owned by a CLT, the governing board will do almost anything to make things right, even to the point of sacrificing the organization itself through a merger or dissolution if that means saving its leaseholders' homes.

III. JUST PLACES: THE TRANSFORMATIVE POTENTIAL OF COMMON GROUND

Long ago, Andre Gorz, a social philosopher living in France, drew a distinction between ameliorative measures that buttress existing relations of property and power versus those that open tiny cracks in the structure of inequality, slowly accumulating over time to offer an ideological and political challenge to the status quo. He called the first "reformist reform" and the second "non-reformist reform."[23]

Gorz's categories were later revived and provocatively applied by James Meehan in his examination of community land trusts in the United States, using the Dudley Street Neighborhood Initiative in Boston as his principal case. He concluded:

> It is clear that CLTs, in their diverse character and situations, walk the fine dividing line between the two tendencies of reformist and non-reformist. In many cases, the CLT legal model has been used as a gimmick to keep low-income housing costs low (thus taking pressure off the state and the private sector). In others, they play a role in raising consciousness to the realities of power in regard to land, questioning speculative owner- ship of land, and enabling some degree of community control over the local land base.[24]

Meehan captures well the tension between the pedestrian, day-to-day practice of CLTs and the loftier, transformative possibilities that may result from their work. CLTs are, in fact, an effective scheme for lowering housing costs, preserving affordability, promoting upkeep, and preventing foreclosures. This full-cycle commitment to cost reduction at the front end and dependable stewardship at the back end is a marked improvement over the build-and-bolt mentality embodied in most other programs for boosting low-income people into homeownership.

At the same time, a community land trust, like every other organization working to improve conditions and to expand opportunities for disadvantaged people, inadvertently reinforces the hold of dominant institutions. When CLTs expand access to mortgage cap- ital for populations and places that have experienced redlining in the past, they contrib- ute to the legitimization of a system of private finance that has been a source of woe for low-income communities, especially communities of color. When CLTs expand access to homeownership for people who have been excluded from the private market, they affirm the individualization of property that has been a flashpoint in the politics of place, where interests of property drive a contentious wedge between owners and renters, and between haves and have-nots. Community land trusts, from this perspective, can be seen as a reformist tool for propping up the status quo, softening the edges of a harmful system that is left unchallenged and unchanged.

There is another way of looking at it, however, for the cumulative effect of community-led development on community-owned land may be to transform that system into something else. An ideology of possessive individualism, used by landlords and homeowners alike to justify their capture of all gains in value accruing to real property, is challenged by a CLT's dogged pursuit of a more equitable balance between the legitimate interests of individual residents and the legitimate interests of the community around them, secured through common ground.[25] The power of private lenders is moderated by the CLT's front-end right to approve all mortgages for buildings sited on its land, screening against predatory lending; it is also blunted by the CLT's back-end right to intervene in cases of mortgage default, preventing most foreclosures. The politics of place are modified by a nonprofit landowner that is drawn into sharing and wielding power on behalf of residents living on and around its land.

Admittedly this happens within the geographic confines of a rather limited territory, encompassing a service area as small as a single neighborhood for some CLTs. It also happens within the functional confines of a limited circle of institutions that determine how land-based wealth is distributed and how real estate is owned, regulated, and financed. Community-owned land may be a creative vehicle for non-reformist reform, but its territorial and institutional reach may not extend very far.[26]

It may be argued, on the other hand, that any institution that offers a counter-narrative to practices and meanings that buttress inequality carries a seed of possibility for influencing a wider circle of places, institutions, and policies. When one community prudently plans for success by improving conditions in a particular place without displacing its most vulnerable residents, it raises the question of why *equitable* development isn't a priority of every neighborhood improvement plan. When community-led development on community-owned land creates a stock of housing that is permanently affordable in the face of market forces that pose a credible threat to all affordably priced housing, most of which would not exist without governmental funds or inclusionary mandates, it raises the question of why *sustainable* development is not a requisite of all housing policy.

A community land trust, from this perspective, represents what Ulrich Beck has called a "creative construction," a social innovation that not only transforms relations within its particular sphere of influence but brings pressure to bear on the intellectual and political systems that surround it, "besieging what exists with a provocative alternative."[27] In a similar vein, Erik Olin Wright has pointed to "community-controlled land trusts" as one of several strategies for achieving what he calls "interstitial transformations." These are alternative institutions that "seek to build new forms of social empowerment in the niches and margins of capitalist society, often where they do not seem to pose any immediate threat to dominant classes and elites."[28]

It cannot be said that most people who are drawn to a CLT, whether as practitioners or beneficiaries, are motivated by the prospect of mounting some sort of ideological, institutional, or political challenge to the status quo. Most have little interest in "besieging" anything. They may be blissfully unaware of the transformative potential of community-owned land beyond its immediate utility in helping low-income people to obtain and retain a home. Even those who passionately embrace the CLT as a vehicle for moving toward a more just society may speak only in whispers about the radical proposition at the heart of the model they employ. As the sweet old lady confided to a colleague of mine several years ago, while talking proudly about the success of her own CLT in doing both urban agriculture and affordable housing on community-owned land, "What we are really about is land reform, but we hide behind the tomatoes."

> "What we are really about is land reform, but we hide behind the tomatoes."

Such reticence is understandable. A community land trust must think twice about calling too much attention to unconventional (and sometimes controversial) elements in its make-up when its leaders must continually beg for grants from public funders, apply for loans from private lenders, and anticipate attacks from reactionary neighbors opposed to anything being built near their own backyards.

Stealth has a price, however. When an innovation like common ground is cautiously kept out the limelight, it is simultaneously kept off the stage, waiting forever in the wings. To move from the periphery to the mainstream, CLTs must be prepared to strut their stuff and prove their worth, confidently proclaiming that *their* way of doing community development is preferable to the way it is normally done. Hiding behind the tomatoes may help a fledgling CLT to get established or may enable a beleaguered CLT to survive, but it does little to demonstrate the comparative advantage of common ground. It hides the fact that community-led development on community-owned land is not "just as good" as more conventional strategies of place-based development. It is better.

It is better because community land trusts are, at heart, more than simply another gimmick for lowering the cost of housing and cultivating a new crop of homeowners. What they are "really about" is equitably and sustainably replanting the contested ground at the intersection of property, power, and place. That may not be something to which all CLT practitioners aspire. That may not be something of which all CLT practitioners speak. But whenever land is controlled by a community within the participatory framework of a CLT, the transformative potential is present to nudge the places where people reside toward greater security and opportunity for all. Common ground provides a versatile platform for promoting development with justice—and justice that lasts.

Notes

1. This chapter is an abbreviated version of an essay published by the *University of San Francisco Law Review* v. 15, no. 1 (2017).

2. An argument for strategies and policies that preserve affordable housing in good economic times and bad can be found in John Emmeus Davis, "Homes that Last: The Case for Counter-Cyclical Stewardship," *Shelterforce* (Winter 2008). Reprinted in J.E. Davis (ed.), *The Community Land Trust Reader* (Cambridge MA: The Lincoln Institute of Land Policy, 2010).

3. While this tradition inevitably invokes images of state confiscation of the estates of a purged aristocracy, there are less draconian examples. The Gramdan Movement in India relied on voluntary donations of land from wealthy landlords in the 1950s. The contemporary land reform movement in Scotland relies on state funds, raised largely through the national lottery, and a 2003 law enacted by the Parliament in Edinburgh that gave communities a first option to purchase the feudal estates on which those communities are sited.

4. An earlier attempt to situate the CLT within the context of different approaches to land reform can be found in John Emmeus Davis, "Reallocating Equity: A Land Trust Model of Land Reform," Pp. 209–232 in *Land Reform, American Style* (Totowa NJ: Rowman & Allanheld, 1984). Reprinted in J.E. Davis (ed.), *The Community Land Trust Reader* (Cambridge MA: The Lincoln Institute of Land Policy, 2010).

5. Evidence for the disparate impact of the mortgage crisis on communities of color can be found in Jacob S. Rugh & Douglas S. Massey, "Racial Segregation and the American Foreclosure Crisis," *American Sociological Review* 75, 2016: 629, 633; and Debbie Gruenstein Bocian, Wei Li, Carolina Reid, & Roberto G. Quercia, *Lost Ground: Disparities in Mortgage Lending and Foreclosures* (Center for Responsible Lending, 2011).

6 Emily Thaden, "Stable Homeownership in a Turbulent Economy: Delinquencies and Foreclosures Remain Low in Community Land Trusts," Working Paper (Cambridge MA: Lincoln Institute of Land Policy, 2011). See also John Emmeus Davis & Alice Stokes, *Lands in Trust, Homes That Last: A Performance Evaluation of the Champlain Housing Trust* (Burlington VT: Champlain Housing Trust, 2009).

7. Penn Loh, "How One Boston Neighborhood Stopped Gentrification in Its Tracks," *YES! Magazine* (January 28, 2015).

8. Jesse A. Myerson, "How to Get Rid of Your Landlord and Socialize American Housing, in Three Easy Steps," *The Nation* (December 8, 2015).

9. The story of DSNI is told by Peter Medoff and Holly Sklar, *Streets of Hope: The Fall and Rise of an Urban Neighborhood* (Boston MA: South End Press, 1994).

10. Rick Jacobus, "The Gentrification Vaccine," *Rooflines* (August 13, 2015).

11. A rise in the value and profitability of a cooperatively-owned enterprise can tempt the firm's shareholders to sell out to an outside buyer, removing the cooperative structure and reaping personal gains, a process known as "demutualization." Just as the leased land beneath a limited-equity housing cooperative can prevent its conversion to a market-rate cooperative or condominiums, a ground lease beneath a worker cooperative or consumer cooperative can give a CLT the ability to prevent demutualization.

12. Ray Oldenburg, *The Great Good Place* (Paragon House, 1989). Quoted at p. 14.

13. Jeffrey Yuen and Greg Rosenberg, "Hanging on to the Land," *Shelterforce* (February 11, 2013). Available at: *http://www.shelterforce.org/article/3068/hanging_on_to_the_land/*

14. To focus on the cost of housing, as I am doing here, is not to ignore the presence of other barriers to geographic mobility, past and present, including discriminatory lending and exclusionary zoning.

15. Jake Blumgart, "Have We Been Wasting Affordable Housing Money?" *Rooflines* (December 3, 2015). Available at: *http://www.shelterforce.org/article/4322/have_we_been_wasting_affordable_housing_money/*. See also: John Emmeus Davis, "Plugging the Leaky Bucket: It's About Time," *Rooflines* (January 27, 2015). Available at: *http://www.rooflines.org/3995/plugging_the_leaky_bucket_its_about_time/*

16. John Emmeus Davis and Rick Jacobus, *The City-CLT Partnership: Municipal Support for Community Land Trusts* (Cambridge MA: Lincoln Institute of Land Policy, 2008).

17. "The overwhelming trend has been for inclusionary housing programs to adopt very long-term affordability periods." Rick Jacobus, *Inclusionary Housing: Creating and Maintaining Equitable Communities* (Cambridge MA: Lincoln Institute of Land Policy, 2015, p. 35).

18. Overviews of these models and mechanisms can be found in John Emmeus Davis, *Shared Equity Homeownership: The Changing Landscape of Resale-Restricted, Owner-Occupied Housing* (Montclair NJ: National Housing Institute, 2006); and Jarrid Green, *Community Control of Land and Housing* (Washington DC: Democracy Collaborative, 2018).

19. That is not to say CLTs ignore the more typical concerns of "sustainable development." Just the opposite. The longer time horizon of the "developer that doesn't go away" makes CLTs more receptive to environmental issues and more attentive to installing durable materials and energy efficient systems than developers who build and bolt.

20. Quote by Devika Goetschius, Executive Director of the Housing Land Trust of Sonoma County, in Emily Thaden and John Emmeus Davis, "Stewardship Works," *Shelterforce* (December 24, 2010). Available at: *http://www.shelterforce.org/article /2080/ stewardship_works/*

21. If the home does go into foreclosure and the lender sells to a buyer that is not a low-income or moderate-income household, the CLT has the option (via the ground lease) of charging that upper-income homebuyer a market-rate ground rent.

22. See, for example, Gharad Bryan, Dean Karlan, & Scott Nelson, "Commitment Devices," *2 Annual Review of Economics 2* (2010); and Colin Camerer, Samuel Issacharoff, George Loewenstein, Ted O'Donoghue, & Matthew Rabin, "Regulation for Conservatives: Behavioral Economics and the Case for 'Asymmetric Paternalism'" *University of Pennsylvania Law Review 151* (2003).

23. Andre Gorz, *Strategy for Labor: A Radical Proposal* (Boston MA: Beacon Press, 1964).

24. James Meehan, "Reinventing Real Estate: The Community Land Trust as a Social Invention in Affordable Housing," *Journal of Applied Social Science 20* (2013, p. 113).

25. From the earliest days of the CLT, its advocates have wrestled with the question of exactly what these "legitimate" interests might be. A seminal discussion of this issue can be found in Institute for Community Economics, *The Community Land Trust Handbook* (Emmaus PA: Rodale Press, 1982). Many other thinkers have wrestled with the same philosophical question. See: R.H. Tawney, *The Acquisitive Society* (New York: Harcourt, Brace and World, 1920); and Reinhold Niebuhr, *The Children of Light and Darkness* (New York: Charles Scribner and Sons, 1944).

26. James DeFilippis, for one, has expressed doubts about CLTs producing society-wide change. While conceding that CLTs "provide a framework for ownership that is both equitable and viable," he notes their lack of an oppositional politics and their limited institutional reach. James DeFilippis, *Unmaking Goliath: Community Control in the Face of Global Capital* (New York: Routledge, 2004). Quote at p. 148.

27. Ulrich Beck, *Individualization: Institutionalized Individualism and Its Social and Political Consequences* (Mike Featherstone ed., 2005). Quote at pp. 190–191.

28. Erik Olin Wright, *Envisioning Real Utopias* (London: Verso, 2010).

3.

Making a Case for CLTs in All Markets, Even Cold Ones

Steve King

The Community Land Trust is a proven tool
for change. When shall we dare use it?[1]
— *Susan Witt and Robert Swann*

Over the past several decades in the United States, there has been a resurgent interest in a certain quality of life afforded by dense urban living, particularly among well-educated, high-income earners. This has precipitated a re-segregation of the population in hot-market metropolitan areas like the one surrounding San Francisco, where housing production has failed to keep pace with economic growth. The persistent, racialized disinvestment and neglect that for decades targeted sections of the Bay Area, including East and West Oakland, Bayview Hunters Point, East Palo Alto, and Richmond, has nearly vanished, as real estate speculators have found opportunities to buy up land and buildings in proximity to downtown San Francisco and Silicon Valley. Long-time working-class residents have been steadily pushed to far-flung exurbs in search of affordability, at the expense of social networks, increased commute times, and diminished cultural connection. Many who remain in the inner Bay Area have been subjected to adverse housing-related by-products of the booming economy, including skyrocketing rents, involuntary displacement, no-fault evictions, tent encampments, and a near paralysis among public officials over how to ameliorate the resulting harm.

This predicament is not unique to the Bay Area, and it is also not shared uniformly across the United States. At the other end of the economic spectrum, many older industrial towns, cities, and regions have experienced a seemingly irreversible downward spiral marked by a long decline of the manufacturing sector, a shrinking middle class, white flight and suburbanization, and the recent foreclosure crisis. Many places that once flourished around specific industries are struggling to survive in the absence of the economic

> We are still lacking a broader argument for why CLTs might be effective in places that are plagued by disinvestment, not reinvestment.

engines that once powered them. Abandonment, high vacancy rates, plummeting home values, municipal fiscal crises, and extreme poverty are but a few of the challenges left in the wake of economic decline. For people living in such cold-market neighborhoods or cities, the prospect of gentrification seems remote, a distant threat that is unlikely ever to materialize.

Urban growth and decline are both uneven and cyclical. If there is one constant about cities in an advanced capitalist economy, it is that they change over time. Indeed, these antipodal cases mask the middling nuances of urban development in post-Industrial American cities. As the urban planner Alan Mallach has noted, even in shrinking, "divided" cities like Detroit, Cleveland, and St. Louis, the investment in high-end, amenity-rich housing is an emergent phenomenon; just a few blocks away from new, upscale development there remains relentless neighborhood decline and poverty.[2]

In hot-market coastal cities and in cold-market metro areas alike, therefore, economic opportunity is not equitably distributed. The benefits of development overwhelmingly accrue to the wealthy, while the burdens disproportionately impact the poor. A similar pattern is found in housing and land use. History is replete with examples of how both public policies and private actions have been divisive, exclusionary, predatory, and destructive, especially for African-American neighborhoods and other communities of color.

Fig. 3.1. Weak-market neighborhood, Old North St. Louis, Missouri, 2014.

A premise and promise of the community land trust model is that it aims straight for the heart of a major cause of these persistent inequities: the ownership and control of land. The fundamental desires for freedom, self-determination, and rootedness *in place* were core motivations for the creation of the first modern CLT in Albany, Georgia nearly fifty years ago. And they remain so today, which is a reason why CLTs are increasingly utilized in neighborhoods and cities with ascending real estate markets. Community activists — and some public officials — see in the CLT a strategic tool to counter the negative externalities of market-driven development that are inflicted disproportionately on low-income households and communities of color. A forceful rhetorical case has been made — and some empirical evidence is beginning to appear — demonstrating that community control of land via a CLT can be an effective hedge against market forces that otherwise displace precariously housed people in disempowered neighborhoods.[3] The development of CLTs in cities like Seattle, Portland, San Francisco, Los Angeles, Denver, Austin, Houston, Washington, DC, Boston, and New York City attests to the allure and applicability of CLTs in ascending markets.

In contrast — and strangely so — a compelling case has never been made for CLTs in cold-market locales, despite the fact that a number of CLTs have succeeded in places where real estate markets are weak.[4] John Emmeus Davis has offered a cogent argument that "counter-cyclical stewardship," the particular forte of CLTs, can be a stabilizing force amidst market fluctuations.[5] We also have some evidence of CLTs bearing out this promise of stability in market troughs, as happened during the foreclosure crisis of 2008–2012 when CLT homeowners did not lose their homes.[6] Nevertheless, we are still lacking a broader argument for why CLTs might be effective in places that are plagued by disinvestment, not reinvestment; that is, places where affordability is not the most pressing issue and where market-instigated displacement is not an imminent threat. This essay is an initial attempt to fill this void, offering a rationale and a provisional menu of strategic options for community control of land via a CLT in cold-market areas.

CHALLENGES AND OPPORTUNITES FOR CLT DEVELOPMENT IN COLD MARKETS

There is a widespread belief amongst practitioners, funders, and institutions in the broader community development and affordable housing fields that the CLT model is neither needed nor workable in cold real estate markets. This reductive conclusion belies an unfortunate misunderstanding of the goals and values of many emerging (and established) CLTs. It is a potentially destructive preconception that can stifle support of new CLT initiatives and thwart important community-driven work before it is given a chance to thrive. Before delving squarely into the qualities of cold-market places and the potential for CLTs in those areas, therefore, it is necessary to consider briefly the question of the relationship between the "strength" of a local real estate market (hot/strong vs. lukewarm/moderate vs. cold/weak) and the prospects for creating a viable CLT.

CLTs operate in a manner that works to correct for defects in both the private market and the broader political system, producing equitable and sustainable outcomes that would not otherwise emerge from either. This ameliorative impact can occur in *any* market. In this respect, the market itself is a precondition for a CLT. If a more just and democratic system was in place that equitably distributed land, housing, and economic opportunity, a CLT might not be needed. In the absence of such a system, however, there is a redistributive and reparative role for CLTs to play, regardless of the relative strength of the local economy and local real estate market.

The feasibility and viability of a CLT in any market — including cold ones — will depend on a complex array of local conditions and factors, including: the type of activities a community is hoping a CLT will undertake; who is invited to (or excluded from) a CLT's decision-making table; and, perhaps most importantly, the presence (or absence) of residents who have organized to improve their neighborhood and to secure a more just allocation of resources. Each of these contingencies offers a window into why a CLT might be the ideal vehicle for equitable development in a cold market.

Cold-market challenges. What are some of the conditions and challenges for doing community development in cold-market areas? By its very nature, a cold-market city or neighborhood suffers from a lack of investment and has relatively little economic activity. Within these geographies, economic opportunity for low-income residents is typically scarce and may lead to declining or unstable populations. The relative lack of private economic activity is often matched, moreover, by limited public investment in services and infrastructure.

> Just because property values have declined in a cold market does not mean that housing tenure is secure.

Spillover effects of a depressed economy are reflected in the built environment. Elevated vacancy levels are a common attribute of cold markets, including both unoccupied or abandoned buildings and vacant or undeveloped land. When vacancy levels climb, the condition and value of the overall building stock begins to deteriorate. Declining property values attract unscrupulous speculators looking to drain the remaining value at the further expense of the building stock and to the detriment of existing residents. This speculative activity is frequently carried out by absentee owners — investors with no connection to the community and no qualms about extracting wealth from struggling residents and their neighborhoods. These conditions invariably put a strain on local government, as property tax revenues wither and the requisite finances for public services begin to evaporate. Public education, infrastructure, public works, parks, and other public facilities — the basic building blocks of civic life — can languish as a result of diminished municipal revenues. Thus begins a vicious, self-reinforcing web of disinvestment and deterioration that is difficult to arrest.

Just because property values have declined in a cold market does not mean that housing tenure is secure. Nor does it mean that housing quality is safe and healthy or that rents are affordable relative to wages. Evictions occur across the entire strong-market/weak-market continuum in the United States, with especially high concentrations in many cold-market areas of the American South, and disproportionate impacts for low-income, African-American, and female-headed households.[7]

While low-income renters are the most vulnerable in this regard, market-rate home-ownership is not necessarily more secure. One indication is the ten million home foreclosures that occurred during the Great Recession, beginning in 2008. Another indication is the enormous number of "severely cost-burdened" homeowners in the United States who earn below the median income for their area and pay more than half their income for housing. In cold-market areas, homeownership might be relatively more affordable for households of modest means, compared to hot-market cities, but it may still be out of reach because wages have stagnated amidst a distressed economy. Moreover, for households who do manage to buy a home in cold-market places, the quality of that housing may be low, especially at the bottom end of the market. And for cost-burdened home-owners, there is usually little money left after paying their monthly housing bills to keep up with necessary repairs.

For residents living in areas where these types of conditions exist, there can be deep physical and psychological trauma, as well as other health-negating influences, including a lack of access to essential services and healthy food options, limited opportunities for sufficient and meaningful work, fractured networks of social capital, poor housing conditions, and overall neighborhood distress. All are fundamental determinants of health and well-being. All tend to deteriorate in a cold-market city or neighborhood where opportunity is restricted.

Cold-market assets. Despite the compounding negative conditions facing residents of cold-market cities and neighborhoods, these places are also replete with many positive and potentially productive assets. The challenge is how to utilize and to leverage those assets in a context of scarcity. Conditions will vary from one place to another, but there are four key assets that may form the basis for CLT development in cold-market areas.

First, land may be plentiful and relatively inexpensive. This is typically one of the most significant barriers to CLT expansion in hot-market areas. By contrast, in cold markets, land that is undeveloped, underutilized, or vacant is often more plentiful — and potentially less costly.

Second, the market demand for buildings (along with land) of any type (residential, commercial, industrial, etc.) is likely suppressed, which may be accompanied by deteriorated physical conditions, tax delinquency, or functional obsolescence. These are not insignificant challenges in terms of liability and the resources needed for acquisition,

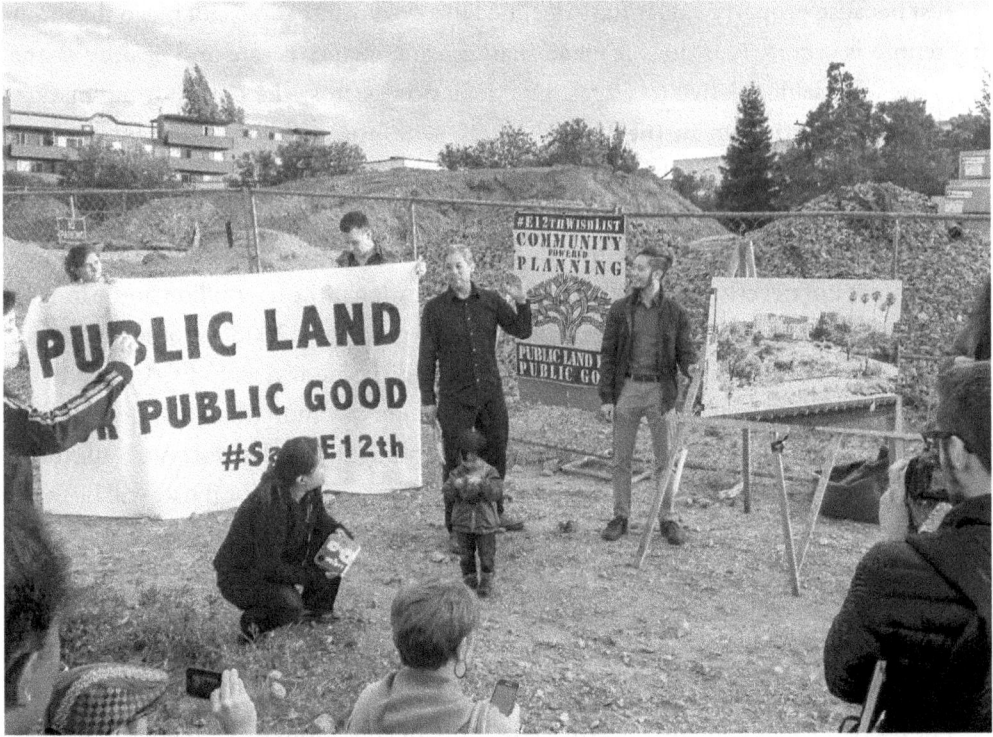

Fig. 3.2. Resident leaders of the East 12th Street Coalition, Oakland, California, demanding community involvement in planning for the redevelopment of land.

rehabilitation, or even demolition, yet a building stock with limited demand and a low cost may still provide an opportunity for CLT development.

Third, people with roots in any place-based community are its most valuable asset. Long-time residents, newcomers, children, families, elders, the displaced, and the house-less — all form the potential base of people-power, waiting to be engaged, to lead, and to craft new solutions to old problems.[8]

Finally, most cold-market places already have a set of community development enti-ties, nonprofit organizations, and faith-based institutions working in and among the com-munity, providing social services and tackling many of the problems noted above. These groups can be sources of financial, technical, and political support for a new CLT. In some cases, a preexisting organization may even take the lead in initiating a CLT or choose to house a fledgling CLT under its corporate umbrella.[9]

These place-based assets provide the opportunity to think expansively about the value and possibilities of the CLT model in areas where the economic rationale around perma-nent affordability — the most frequently touted benefit of CLTs — is less than compel-ling due to prevailing market conditions. If the looming loss of housing affordability as a market feature is not a pressing issue, however, then why else might a community want to consider creation of a CLT? Some strategic possibilities are considered below.

BEYOND HOMEOWNERSHIP: EXPLORING THE MYRIAD OPTIONS FOR COMMUNITY-OWNED LAND IN COLD MARKETS

One of the most powerful attributes of the CLT model is its versatility; it is deployable across a range of land uses and societal needs, as identified by its community. Yet, this broad applicability has been underutilized as CLTs have grown in popularity for a primary use: affordable housing in general, and owner-occupied housing in particular.

> Community-led development on community-owned land is the essence of a CLT.

The scant attention paid to CLT development in cold-market areas, therefore, may derive in part from the manner in which the field has advanced over the past several decades. CLTs have become largely synonymous with the production and stewardship of *permanently affordable homeownership*. This is undoubtedly an important and laudable achievement. But narrowing the model's focus to a single purpose has resulted in minimizing the importance of a more fundamental building block: community-owned and community-governed land. Indeed, it can be argued that community-led development on community-owned land is the essence of a CLT, rather than the permanent affordability of owner-occupied housing. The former is *the* feature that connects the CLT of today to the founders of New Communities, Inc. and their struggle for justice, liberation, and self-determination.[10]

The framework of community-led development on community-owned land forms the basis for considering the strategic potential of CLTs in cold-market areas. It provides an opening to explore nascent possibilities for project development and collective action that are currently under-examined and undervalued in the burgeoning CLT field, at least in the United States. Beyond permanently affordable homeownership, the range of opportunity for CLTs is extensive. Many housing-oriented CLTs have, in fact, already expanded their purviews to include projects with non-residential land uses, with affiliated or mission-supporting lines of business. A cursory look at some of these expansive uses and creative possibilities will help to demonstrate the potential for community-owned land in cold-market areas.

Community Gardens, Sustainable Agriculture, and Open Space

One of the most common non-residential uses of CLT land has been for food production. This option may be particularly relevant in low-income, cold-market neighborhoods where access to fresh and healthy food is often limited. There are plentiful examples of existing CLTs that steward land for growing food and food-related businesses.[11] These range from small infill community gardens to multi-acre farms and large-scale open space and agricultural land conservation. In cold-market areas where vacant land may be relatively accessible (either via fee simple ownership or long-term leasing arrangements managed by a CLT), small-scale urban agriculture or community gardening can serve as a catalytic starting point for new organizations that may not yet have the capacity or resources to undertake larger or costlier real estate projects. Additionally, the activation of an underutilized or problematic parcel with neighborhood residents and partners can serve as a powerful community-building and organizing vehicle to develop goodwill, awareness, and support for additional activities on community-owned land.

As one example, the first property acquired by the Parkdale Neighbourhood Land Trust (PNLT) in Toronto, Canada was a site for gardening, and has served as a successful precursor to other CLT acquisitions. In 2017, PNLT acquired the 7,000 square-foot Milky Way Garden parcel to be permanently preserved as a community-controlled asset. The site plays a particularly vital role for newcomers from Tibet to build community and to grow culturally-appropriate produce. The campaign to acquire the lot also played a galvanizing role to raise funds from community residents and to bolster awareness of the mission of the CLT. PNLT owns the lot and is active in facilitating the community vision for the parcel, leasing the land to a partner organization to manage on a day-to-day basis.

On a much larger scale, the Athens Land Trust (ALT) in Athens, Georgia has established an impressive program of land conservation and community agriculture in addition to their affordable housing work. As of 2017, the Athens Land Trust had protected 16,485 acres of land in 36 Georgia counties via both conservation easements and ownership. These holdings included "natural habitats and river frontage, working agricultural land and land of historical significance, and land for public recreation."[12] Additionally, ALT's vibrant community agricultural program provides much-needed access to land — as well as programmatic support — for growing food and food-related businesses. As a steward of land across a diverse range of uses, ALT utilizes these assets to create programs

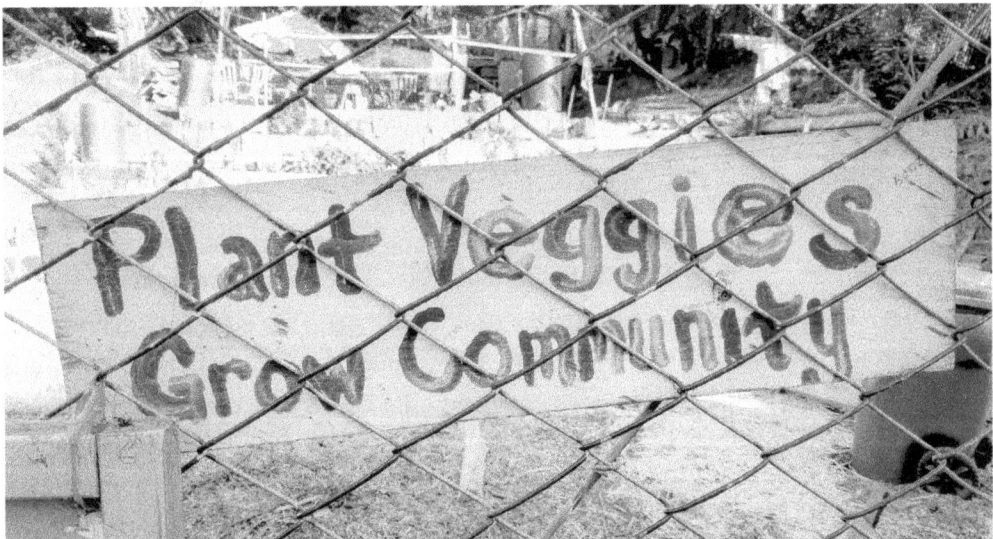

Fig. 3.3. Community garden, Oakland, California.

offering paid career development and training opportunities for young people in the construction trades, urban farming, and land conservation—all with an eye toward nurturing future generations of local leadership around land-based justice and opportunity.

Commercial Land Uses

Commercial uses for community-owned land span an incredibly diverse mix of options and scales. The possibilities are endless, limited only by what a community can envision and by what a municipality will permit according to its zoning and building codes. In the commercial context, as with other CLT land tenure arrangements, a CLT can play the foundational role of acquiring land and leasing it out to support community-prioritized economic development, or the CLT can own and manage both the land and the improvements.[13] Existing commercial CLT uses include not only stewarding land and buildings for mission-aligned nonprofit and community-serving organizations, but also for more unusual uses such as a gas station in a rural California coastal community (the Bolinas CLT's Bo-Gas) and a mobile meat-processing facility in rural Washington State (Lopez CLT).

In cold-market areas, a CLT might play a particularly valuable role in supporting non-residential strategies that produce targeted economic benefits and job opportunities for residents who have been harmed by disinvestment. To cite an example from another country, the Homebaked CLT in Liverpool, England got started in 2012 as a reaction to a top-down, government-initiated urban renewal plan to demolish a swath of historic buildings in the neighborhood of Anfield.[14] In response, residents coalesced around a vision to save a cherished neighborhood bakery, turning it into a cooperatively owned business. The Homebaked CLT was established to acquire the bakery building and to implement a community-led vision for redeveloping the neighborhood's commercial district. Saving the bakery served as the catalyzing project by: initiating the CLT; preserving a visible anchor business; and laying the groundwork for a more expansive agenda for community-owned land in the neighborhood.

Back in the USA, the Lopez CLT in Washington State serves as the steward for a number of commercial storefronts that provide incubator space for small, local businesses. All twelve of the businesses that utilize these spaces are owned by homeowner-leaseholders of the Lopez CLT. Connecting economic and housing security, these commercial spaces offer CLT residents an opportunity to build individual assets in ways that do not put their homes at risk, while generating local economic benefits that circulate within the community.

Subsidiary, Affiliated, and Mutually-Supporting Businesses

Across the national landscape, there are more and more cases of CLTs creating affiliated entities or businesses that either bolster the work of the CLT or create aligned opportunities for CLT residents and members. For instance, both Proud Ground, a CLT in

Portland, Oregon, and the Northern California Land Trust in Berkeley, California have established real estate brokerages to support in-house property transactions and to generate revenue for the CLT through non-CLT transactions. One Roof Community Housing, a CLT in Duluth, Minnesota has set up a subsidiary firm to do construction and home rehabilitation for the parent organization. In Berkeley and Oakland, California, three CLTs have come together to explore the creation of a worker-owned property management cooperative to support the needs of resident-operated CLT properties, housing cooperatives, worker cooperatives, and other aligned organizations. It is envisioned that the property management cooperative will leverage the skills of existing CLT residents and co-op worker-owners to provide basic property management services as well as capacity building among a broad network of allied organizations.

CLT as Steward and Supporter of Community Health and Stability

As John Emmeus Davis has reminded us, the stewardship function of a CLT is not just about maintaining affordability — it also includes the preservation of housing *quality* and *security*.[15] Even in markets where affordability may not be a pressing concern, there are important roles a CLT can play in supporting residents with maintenance, repair, and overall housing quality, as well as intervening to cure defaults, advocating for better public policies and services with and for CLT homeowners and tenants, and preventing displacement via foreclosure or eviction.

Some of these services may also be offered to non-CLT residents, particularly in areas where such services are lacking. Many existing CLTs, for example, already provide pre- and post-purchase homeowner education, credit counseling, and income and asset development coaching for anyone living within their service area, regardless of whether they are CLT homeowners. Depending upon what is needed in a community, a CLT might offer home repair and maintenance support, small business coaching and loans, tenant legal services, and various forms of renter, homebuyer, homeowner, and homelessness assistance.[16]

BEYOND DEVELOPMENT:
PLANNING, ORGANIZING, AND BUILDING POWER

In cold-market areas where housing affordability is not a priority issue, there may still be significant barriers to engagement, democratic participation, and decision-making related to intersecting economic, political, and ecological issues that disproportionately impact low-income residents and people of color. For these reasons, the resident-centered governance structure of a CLT can serve as a hub to meaningfully assess, analyze, and advance the needs of those struggling most severely in a cold market. Further, a CLT can be a potent vehicle for leadership development, resident organizing, and base-building as a precursor to actually pursuing community-led real estate activities.[17] Community organizing and base-building can, in turn, help to nurture the conditions in which a CLT emerges, grows, and thrives. An organized cohort of resident leaders and CLT members can hold elected officials accountable, exert political pressure when needed, and wield the people-power required to evidence a demand for community-led development on community-owned land.

The Dudley Street Neighborhood Initiative (DSNI) — and its affiliated CLT, Dudley Neighbors, Inc. (DNI) — in the Roxbury section of Boston provide instructive examples of community organizing and base-building in what was once a cold-market neighborhood. DNI is frequently touted as one of the most successful community land trusts in the United States, although few other CLTs have taken up their intentional model of broad-based resident empowerment and community-led planning and development. That approach to community development remains as audacious today as it was in 1984 when DSNI was founded.[18]

From the outset, DSNI was strategically oriented to support two core activities: place-based organizing of neighborhood residents and resident-led visioning and planning. When combined with the organization's affiliated community land trust, these activities comprised the productive inputs for enacting a community-building strategy on community-owned and community-controlled land.[19] This approach remains particularly vital because it puts the leadership of existing residents at the center of a strategy that builds

Fig. 3.4. Alliance of Californians for Community Empowerment. Oakland CLT homeowners, Shekinah Samaya-Thomas and Chris Thomas, join Vanessa Bulnes (with megaphone), advocating for resident-controlled housing on community-owned land.

upon both individual and community capacities and assets. In cities and neighborhoods where low-income residents and communities of color have been systematically disempowered and traumatized by market activity and public policy, this is a fundamental first step toward a restorative, just, and equitable redistribution of power. As Gus Newport, DSNI's former executive director, has observed:

> To successfully redevelop neighborhoods which have become blighted through years of neglect due to bank "redlining," failed government programs and poor planning, the only way that these areas can be turned around is with the will and involvement of concerned neighbors. A true foundation which will assure long term participation and neighborhood stabilization only happens when people can see and feel that their involvement and control (empowerment) is real. Anything short of this will result in additional failure, which is what we have in the majority of inner cities across the United States.[20]

BEYOND THE COLD-MARKET PRESENT: PLANNING FOR A JUST AND EQUITABLE FUTURE

Market Conditions Change: Safeguarding the Future

For people affiliated with CLTs in warm-market or hot-market areas, it is common to wistfully ponder an alternate reality in which the CLT might have emerged a decade or two earlier, when land and housing cost a fraction of current prices. By contrast, in cold-market areas, few people can imagine a future reality when costs will soar and a wave of investment and high-end development will threaten to displace low-income and moderate-income residents who are presently there. How can these two disparate perspectives be reconciled?

History serves as a guide on a specific point related to the failure of markets to provide for those most in need and the inability of political institutions to anticipate or to pre-emptively set the stage for truly equitable outcomes from development. Disinvestment has often been a precursor to new waves of private investment in stagnant real estate markets. The priority of government officials in such situations is often to incentivize *any* investment in housing or commercial development, rather than risk scaring investors away by requiring the benefits of development to be shared with residents who are most in need.

Equitable development is possible, but it must be coaxed into existence with political pressure and inclusive, democratic participation. This provides a basic rationale for building the infrastructure of a CLT in the absence of an imminent threat of displacement. Quite simply, local residents, who are often excluded from participating in development decisions, deserve a seat at the table. In many communities, the only way to assert this right is to organize, to build community power, to demand accountability, and to take control of development under the collective formation of a CLT.

There is also a need for a more nuanced understanding of the profound temporal balancing act in which CLTs are engaged. CLTs hold land for community benefit for a very long time. While CLTs and their members enact programs that address immediate resident-identified needs, CLTs must simultaneously uphold an extraordinary long-term vision for land reform and social justice. This delicate balance of community priorities across different timelines is a rarely acknowledged and woefully underappreciated hallmark of the CLT. In a cold market, the organizational container to hold land and to promote equitable development across a longer arc of time may reveal new avenues for pursuing community resilience and sustainability.

Markets Are the Problem:
Planning for a Future We Actually Want

Given the legacy and persistence of racial discrimination in housing and urban development and the disparate impact of development on specific populations, it is practical for a historically deprived and disempowered community to demand more control over the ownership, use, and development of land. In cold-market areas, in particular, it is both logical and strategic to pursue alternative solutions rather than the same top-down, market-reliant approaches that have harmed, disenfranchised, and marginalized communities in the past.

There is a growing cohort of community development organizers and practitioners who view the common stewardship of land as part of a fundamental bridge to an emancipatory future that will supplant the current market-based system. These explicitly visionary, transformational, and political efforts are ambitious roadmaps for a *just transition* to a more equitable, healthy, and sustainable future.[21]

Cooperation Jackson in Jackson, Mississippi provides an especially compelling example of a comprehensive project for sustainable, resident-led development, economic democracy, and community ownership. Jackson is a city that exhibits many features of a cold market. The organizers of Cooperation Jackson understand, however, that should the local economy eventually improve through market-based approaches, the needs of Jackson's black and brown residents are unlikely to be met.

Kali Akuno of Cooperation Jackson sees a strategic opportunity in the fact that Jackson's economy is presently depressed. It creates "breathing room" on the margins to envision and to enact a grand plan for a better, more just future. In his words:

> We harness this breathing room by exploiting the fact that there is minimal competition in the area to serve as a distraction or dilution of our focus, a tremendous degree of pent-up social demand waiting to be fulfilled and a deep reservoir of unrealized human potential waiting to be tapped.[22]

Along with a solidarity network of democratically-run, worker-owned cooperative enterprises, Cooperation Jackson has developed the Fannie Lou Hamer Community Land Trust as a core element of its long-term vision for developing and sustaining a new economic base for local residents. The importance of bringing more land into the CLT is one of long-term survival in the face of ongoing racial discrimination and economic austerity. As Akuno has said: "If the land shifts, the power shifts."[23]

Restoring Indigenous Land Stewardship

For those who come to the CLT in search of a model for land-based justice, many believe that the only way to achieve a truly just and equitable future will be to acknowledge and to repair the centuries of harm that have been inflicted upon indigenous peoples through colonial systems of enclosure, exclusion, and expropriation of tribal lands.

Fig. 3.5. Rammay Garden, Sogorea Te Land Trust, West Oakland, California, 2019.

Indigenous women leaders of the Sogorea Te Land Trust in Northern California provide one example. They are developing a new pathway to return ancestral Chochenyo and Karkin Ohlone lands to indigenous stewardship. Their vision is to restore sacred Ohlone land to a state that precedes and transcends the market-based system of private property. The leaders of the Sogorea Te Land Trust are seeding a transformative conversation that invites all residents of the Bay Area to reevaluate their relationship to the land they inhabit and to acknowledge that indigenous people co-inhabit their ancestral homelands alongside non-native residents, despite a contested history.

CLTs everywhere have an important role to play as allies in support of indigenous land struggles. In the particular context of cold markets, one potential avenue for advocacy resides in the re-conveyance of land that has been cheapened in terms of market logic, but may hold deep religious or cultural value for indigenous peoples.

In some cold-market neighborhoods, cities, and regions, a depressed economy with devalued real estate may present a unique opportunity, where a restorative conversation around returning land to indigenous stewardship could take root.

—

CONCLUSION

Even in stable markets with established CLTs, private and public support for community-led development on community-owned land often remains tenuous. The model has yet to gain the broad-based acceptance it deserves, despite the stellar performance of CLTs to date.[24] Given that many CLTs work exclusively in communities of color and that most CLT housing is developed for low-income households, the inequitable distribution of resources to support the development and expansion of affordable housing on CLT land must necessarily be viewed as a racial and economic justice issue. This is a reality affecting hot, cold, and lukewarm markets alike.

> The lack of resources being made available for the expansion of CLTs in the USA is due less to what a CLT is, than to who it benefits.

The lack of resources being made available for the expansion of CLTs in the USA is due less to what a CLT *is,* than to *who* it benefits. It is a reflection of how deeply entrenched the current system of housing delivery remains; how little room there is for models of tenure that push beyond the reductive dichotomy of renting versus owning; and how little political will there is to reform that system to allow more just forms of landownership to flourish in all markets.

CLTs continue to be criticized by skeptics for "not getting to scale," measured solely in terms of the number of housing units in a CLT's portfolio. A rejoinder to this narrow conception of scale has been offered by Zachary Murray of the Oakland CLT, who points out that many grassroots CLTs are seeking to elevate something far more fundamental: community control of land in places where, for generations, residents have been denied any sort of collective control over how land has been used or developed. It can also be said that scale should be measured *horizontally,* counting the number of communities that have adopted strategies that put land use decision-making and long-term control in the hands of residents who have been systematically and historically cut out of the frame.

To date, cold-market cities and neighborhoods have been an overlooked part of the horizontal potential and performance of CLTs. As the CLT model continues the long journey towards acceptance and professionalization, however, there exists an opportunity to apply the model in places and ways that go beyond its current hot-market focus on preserving the affordability of owner-occupied housing. In this context, cold markets are prime areas for CLT invention and exploration. They provide opportunities for community-led development on community-owned land that include more than housing;

opportunities to build resilient models of democratic participation and governance through which residents can influence current and *future* development; and opportunities to restore land justice in communities that have been harmed by government policy, market activity, and white supremacy. The road may be rockier in cold markets, but the long-term growth, vitality, and acceptance of the CLT movement demands a model that is inclusive and deployable in any market.

Notes

1. Susan Witt and Robert Swann, "Land: Challenge and Opportunity," Schumacher Center for a New Economics, May 1995. (*https://centerforneweconomics.org/publications/land-challenge-and-opportunity/*).

2. Alan Mallach, *The Divided City: Poverty and Prosperity in Urban America* (Washington, DC: Island Press, 2018).

3. Myungshik Choi, Shannon Van Zandt, and David Matarrita-Cascante, "Can community land trusts slow gentrification?" *Journal of Urban Affairs,* 40:3, 394–411 (2018).

4. Various terms are used throughout this essay to refer to cold-market areas, including struggling, declining, weak, divided, declining, or shrinking — mainly echoing the range of descriptors used in the voluminous literature on urban decline. Admittedly, these terms are imprecise and not necessarily synonyms. Note, too, that this essay does not take a position on geographic scale, recognizing that weak-market dynamics are relative and can play out at the neighborhood, city, and/or regional level.

5. John Emmeus Davis, "Homes That Last," *Shelterforce,* National Housing Institute, December 2008 (*https://shelterforce.org/2008/12/22/homes_that_last/*).

6. Emily Thaden, "Stable Home Ownership in a Turbulent Economy: Delinquencies and Foreclosures Remain Low in Community Land Trusts," Lincoln Institute of Land Policy, Working Paper WP11ET1, July 2011.

7. Max Blau, "Black Southerners Are Bearing the Brunt of America's Eviction Epidemic," Stateline [online], January 18, 2019 (*https://www.pewtrusts.org/en/research-and-analysis/blogs/stateline/2019/01/18/black-southerners-are-bearing-the-brunt-of-americas-eviction-epidemic*). T. Cookson, et. al., *Losing Home: The Human Cost of Eviction in Seattle,* A Report by the Seattle Women's Commission and the Housing Justice Project of the King County Bar Association, September 2018 (*https://www.seattle.gov/Documents/Departments/SeattleWomensCommission/LosingHome_9-18-18.pdf*). Matthew Desmond, "Poor Black Women Are Evicted at Alarming Rates, Setting Off a Chain of Hardship," MacArthur Foundation Policy Research Brief, March 2014 (*https://www.macfound.org/media/files/HHM_Research_Brief_-_Poor_Black_Women_Are_Evicted_at_Alarming_Rates.pdf*).

8. The "displaced" are included here because there are many instances of people maintaining connections to neighborhoods from which they've been displaced. Folks who have been forced to move away from a neighborhood in which their families may have lived for several generations, frequently make the trek back to attend church, to shop, or to see family and friends. Many would welcome the chance to return — and a CLT might be a vehicle to facilitate their return. A handful of cities have adopted "right to return" policies or given housing preferences for displaced residents.

9. Existing groups can also be gatekeepers to accessing essential resources and knowledge or can be dismissive of innovative ideas and approaches — both common reactions to new CLT efforts in areas where the model is unfamiliar.

10. "Community-led development on community-owned land" aka "common ground" is John Davis' phrasing. John Emmeus Davis, "Common Ground: Community-Owned Land as a Platform for Equitable and Sustainable Development," *University of San Francisco Law Review,* Vol 51, No. 1, 2014.

11. Greg Rosenberg and Jeffrey Yuen have surveyed the field and compiled a useful compendium of both agricultural and commercial CLT projects. See Greg Rosenberg and Jeffrey Yuen, "Beyond Housing: Urban Agriculture and Commercial Development by Community Land Trusts," Lincoln Institute of Land Policy, Working Paper WP13GR1, 2012.

12. Athens Land Trust, "2017 Annual Report." (*https://athenslandtrust.org/wp-content/uploads/2019/01/2017-Annual-Report-1.2.19-1.pdf*).

13. For a discussion of opportunities and challenges for commercial CLT applications, see: Elizabeth Sorce, "The Role of Community Land Trusts in Preserving and Creating Commercial Assets: A Dual Case Study of Rondo CLT in St. Paul, Minnesota and Crescent City CLT in New Orleans, Louisiana" (2012). University of New Orleans Theses and Dissertations. Paper 1501 (*http://scholarworks.uno.edu/td/1501*).

14. See the Homebaked CLT website for more information: *http://homebaked.org.uk/about/we_are_homebaked/*

15. John Emmeus Davis, "Homes That Last," op. cit.

16. Services that are offered to residents who do not live in CLT housing may enable a CLT to diversify its revenues, gaining access to new sources funding.

17. Many CLTs adopt strong community organizing and political strategies in advance of — or alongside — actual real estate development work. For instance, TRUST South LA has a vibrant resident-centered transportation and mobility justice program that advocates for healthy, walkable, and "bikeable" streets — a major quality-of-life issue

for residents of this Los Angeles neighborhood. In New Orleans, the Jane Place Neighborhood Sustainability Initiative has advanced a robust advocacy agenda around the impacts of short-term rentals (such as AirBnB) on the growing affordability crisis, as a separate yet related component of their CLT work.

18. For a history of the early years of DSNI, see Peter Medoff and Holly Sklar, *Streets of Hope: The Fall and Rise of an Urban Neighborhood* (Boston, MA: South End Press, 1999) and *Holding Ground: The Rebirth of Dudley Street* [Video], directed by Mark Lipman and Leah Mahan, Holding Ground Productions, 1997.

19. Dudley Street Neighborhood Initiative, *From the Bottom Up: The Dudley Street Neighborhood Initiative Strategy for Sustainable Economic Development,* Unpublished Draft Manuscript, November 1997.

20. Eugene "Gus" Newport, *The Dudley Street Neighborhood Initiative, Roxbury, Massachusetts: History and Observations,* Unpublished Manuscript, July 1991.

21. On the concept of "just transition," see Movement Generation Justice and Ecology Project, *From Banks and Tanks to Cooperation and Caring: A Strategic Framework for a Just Transition.* (*https://movementgeneration.org/wp-content/uploads/2016/11/JT_booklet_Eng_printspreads.pdf*).

22. Kali Akuno, "Build and Fight: The Program and Strategy of Cooperation Jackson," in Cooperation Jackson (Kali Akuno, Sacajawea Hall, and Brandon King) and Ajamu Nangwaya (eds.), *Jackson Rising: The Struggle for Economic Democracy and Black Self-Determination in Jackson, Mississippi,* Daraja Press, 2017.

23. Hazel Sheffield, "Cooperation Jackson on How to Build an Alternative Economy for People of Colour," The Independent UK, May 31, 2019 (*https://www.independent.co.uk/news/business/indyventure/cooperation-jackson-solidarity-economy-neoliberalism-alternatives-a8936801.html*).

24. This has been correctly characterized as a new form of redlining — a systemic bias in both the government and finance sectors that are connected to real estate, housing, and social programs. See: John Emmeus Davis, "A New Kind of Redlining: Punishing Success," *Shelterforce,* May 6, 2013 (*https://shelterforce.org/2013/05/06/a_new_kind_of_redlining_punishing_success/*).

4.

A Reflection on the Bioethics
of Community Land Trusts

María E. Hernández-Torrales

That the house of every one is to him as his
castle and fortress as well for defense against
injury and violence, as for his repose . . .
—*Sir Edward Coke (1552–1634), English judge and jurist*

Housing is a topic that invites us and summons us. It invites us to reflect on the meaning of housing with regard to the development of human beings. It also summons us to act, moving from passive reflection to active intervention in order to secure the well-being of those who lack the means to satisfy the fundamental right to housing. We shall focus here on the community land trust (CLT), a nonprofit organization that is built around the strategy of acquiring and holding land for the purpose of satisfying the common needs of a place-based community such as the provision of land for affordable housing or for farming and food security. The CLT can be analyzed from two basic perspectives. The first perspective is organizational, examining the structure that ensures that a CLT's objectives are met. The second perspective is moral, pertaining to the values that move human beings to work for other human beings who lack fundamental rights such as the right to housing and food.

Our attention will be directed mostly toward this last perspective, demonstrating that the CLT is an ethical model to pursue. We will analyze the moral values that inspire community-based nonprofit organizations to embrace this practice, motivating them to establish a CLT. We will use a bioethical analysis, a comprehensive perspective that takes into consideration not only the needs and development of human beings, but also our relationship with everything that surrounds us as inhabitants of a planet where resources are finite. By examining the CLT model from a bioethical standpoint, we focus predominantly on the balance between the personal interests of individuals and the collective interests through which a community is formed. From this standpoint, we conclude and affirm that the CLT is an ethical model, one imbued with a particular set of values pertaining to satisfaction of a right to housing and a right to a decent life. In this regard, a CLT walks a path and reaches a destination that is distinct and separate from the path typically followed by a fragmented and individualist society.

BIOETHICS AS A TOOL FOR ANALYSIS AND REFLECTION

In the essay "The Land Ethic" of his classic book, *A Sand County Almanac*, Aldo Leopold (1949) reflected on how human beings are part of a bigger ecological system and how, together, characteristics of the Earth and of the people who inhabit it determine the course of historical events. Additionally, all ethics are sustained by the belief that every individual is a member of a community composed of interdependent parts; accordingly, an individual's ethics, guiding personal action in complicated or new situations, move him or her toward collaboration with other community members.

> Bioethics advocates a concept of progress that places an equal emphasis on the individual and the collective.

The term "bioethics" was coined in 1971 by Van Rensselaer Potter in his monograph *Bioethics: Bridge to the Future*. The publication's lofty purpose was to contribute to the future of humanity by uniting two cultures, science and humanities, through the formation of a new discipline which he named *bioethics* (Potter, 1971). Potter stated that all ethics imply action aligned with moral standards. He specified that it is necessary to remember that ethics have to be accompanied by a realistic understanding of the relationships amongst all living creatures and the environment in which they live in — ecology, in its broadest sense. Ethical values cannot be separated from biological facts.

Potter also argued that "[w]e are in great need for a Land Ethic, a Wildlife Ethic, a Population Ethic, a Consumption Ethic, an Urban Ethic, an International Ethic, a Geriatric Ethic, and so on . . . All of them involve Bioethics." There are many problematic situations that we encounter as a society, including limited resources like water and energy, the pressures of population growth and an aging population, the lack of adequate and decent housing, our disrespect and damage of nature, global warming and climate change. In the face of these many problems, scientific knowledge and philosophical values have to be combined and transcribed into practical wisdom, so that knowledge can be used to address holistic human needs. Knowledge has to strengthen the individual, while simultaneously strengthening society. Bioethics advocates a concept of progress that places an equal emphasis on the individual and the collective. Individual progress and societal progress are interdependent and, ideally, they are pursued in such a way as to be equitably and sustainably in balance (Potter, 1971).

Over the course of its forty-eight years of existence, bioethics has become one of the most highly developed fields in the study of applied ethics. A major contribution was made to bioethics by Tom Beauchamp and James Childress (1979), according to Professor Jorge José Ferrer (2016, 97), when they proposed four general principles as the basic pillars on which a bioethical analysis could be built: (1) respect for the autonomy of our choices; (2) non-maleficence; (3) beneficence; and (4) distributive justice.[1] As discussed by Professor Ferrer, these principles do not establish specific standards for all the situations we face daily, but by using the principles as a basic framework for deliberation, we can generate the precise details that will guide our actions in a situation at hand (Ibid., 71). Within this framework, according to Diego Garcia, the deliberation process should take into consideration facts, conflicted values, the course of action or duty, and finally, the best solution that is also in accordance with norms established by the law (Seoane, 2016, 493).

Respect for the *autonomy* of our choices assumes that our actions are taken freely and with informed consent. To determine if any given action is autonomous, it has to be intentional, understood, and free from external controls or influences. *Non-maleficence* entails an intentional abstention from causing harm. *Beneficence* requires us to contribute to the well-being of others and to act positively on their behalf. *Distributive justice* is based on the fair distribution of scarce resources. A material principle of distributive justice is based on the fair distribution of scarce resources, providing everyone with the material means to develop essential capabilities for a productive life (Ferrer, 2006).

THE RIGHT TO HOUSING

Housing that is decent, affordable, and secure is one of the key factors in the life of every human being. It is a social determinant of health (Hernández, 2016). In the words of the Supreme Court of the United States (*Block v. Hirsch,* 256 US 135, 156 [1921]): "Housing is a necessary of life." Without housing, it is not possible to exercise any other right. Mathew Desmond (2016, 293) has argued that housing is the center of life: it is the shelter where we rest from all external pressures, the place where we can be ourselves. He adds that housing creates psychological stability, which permits people to invest in their homes and in their social relationships (Ibid, 296). It is also a crucial element for young people to achieve academic excellence and to complete their studies. The stability that housing provides to individuals and to families is the basis for a supportive community where residents are in control. The opposite is also true. When families or individuals lack decent, affordable and secure housing, they tend also to lack stability in their homes, family life, neighborhood, school, job, and possessions.

Housing is such an important matter that it is included in the International Declaration of Human Rights,[2] adopted by the United Nations in 1948. Article 25 declared housing to be one of the necessary components for a decent and adequate life (UN, 1948, Art. 25). Within the framework of human rights, housing is related to solidarity in the sense that people live in homes, but they are also part of a neighborhood and part of a community, with an established social fabric and their own web of relations. We can infer, therefore, that housing is an overarching concept that surpasses the physical aspects of a living space (Madden, 2017). Safe, decent, affordable housing gives people the stability and ability to build durable social networks and to live in vibrant communities.

In October 2016, the Third UN World Conference on Housing and Sustainable Urban Development (Habitat III), held in Quito, Ecuador, endorsed the *New Urban Agenda* (ONU, 2017). Basing itself on the estimate that by 2030, six out of 10 people will live in cities, the *New Urban Agenda* highlights the relationship between urbanization and equitable development, where the politics and strategies of urban renovation are intertwined with the creation of jobs, expanded opportunities for generating a livelihood, and the improvement of quality of life (ONU, 2017, iv). Housing is at the center of the *New Urban Agenda*, as it is in another UN document, the *2030 Agenda for Sustainable Development and the Objectives for Sustainable Goals (SDGs)*. Sustainable Development Goal 11, §11.1. seeks to ensure that by 2030 all people will have access to adequate, safe and affordable housing, access to basic services, and all slums will have been improved (ONU, 2015).

Despite international acknowledgement of the importance of housing, however, recognized by sovereign countries and the United Nations alike, the reality experienced by millions of people around the world contradicts this acknowledgement. According to Clerc (2016), forty years after the first Habitat Conference (Habitat I), which became the foundation for the UN's Habitat Program, close to 100 million people now reside in substandard settlements or live on the streets. Stigmatized and negatively stereotyped, these people are deprived of essential services and basic infrastructure. Millions of others have been displaced, stripped of their homes due to inadequate planning or disasters associated with climate change (UN High Commissioner for Refugees, 2019); or they have been forced to live in refugee camps as a result of war or discriminatory public policies (Newey, 2019). Numerous people who *do* have a roof over their heads are forced to live in a disgraceful and inadequate manner as a result of poverty, inequity, discrimination, and environmental injustice (Clerc, 2016).

> When land and housing are viewed as commodities, they are far from being treated as a human right.

There are also many communities of low-income people who live in constant fear of being displaced because of market pressures. This is especially true in informal settlements where hundreds, sometimes thousands, of people are living on land to which they have neither a secure right of ownership nor a secure right of use.[3] Similarly, extreme natural events like hurricanes, floods, wildfires, rising seas, or droughts can cause the involuntary displacement of low-income people, who are then prevented from returning and rebuilding by a combination of public policy and private speculation by "disaster capitalists" who have snatched up newly cleared land.

Many developed and underdeveloped countries treat land and housing as luxuries for those who can pay the price. They become objects of speculation, unlimited accumulation, and wealth generation. When land and housing are viewed in such a way — i.e., as private commodities rather than common necessities — they are far from being treated as a human right (Farha, 2018).

HOUSING AS A CAUSE OF SEGREGATION AND DISCRIMINATION

There is a crisis in housing that affects people all over the world. The bioethical analysis presented in this essay is valid wherever the inadequacy of housing exists, affecting individuals and families in many countries. For the purposes of the current analysis, we will focus on the housing situation and its trajectory in the United States.

Discriminatory practices in the USA have been manifested in all spheres, public and private, but especially in the production, financing, and regulation of housing. In his important book, *The Color of Law: A Forgotten History of How Our Government Segregated America*, Richard Rothstein (2017) describes how the federal government developed housing during World War I for individuals working in defense-related industries; that is, for those who worked in shipyards and ammunition plants. The 83 housing projects that were developed by the government across 26 different states were occupied by 170,000 white workers and their families. Black workers were excluded from these housing projects, even from those developed close to industrial sites where black people represented a significant percentage of the workforce. During the same period, policies established by the federal government and by state governments imposed segregationist practices, forcing black people to live in overcrowded slums, far from city centers and employment opportunities (Rothstein, 2017). Urban planners designed neighborhoods that were reserved for white people. The black population was intentionally excluded or removed from those areas.

During World War II, the housing shortage became acute for both low-income and moderate-income families in the United States. As a response, the New Deal policies implemented by Franklin Delano Roosevelt led to the creation of the first public housing projects for civilians who were not part of a defense program. Race determined the program's design. Separate housing projects were built for black people, who were completely excluded from projects designated for white people. In the rare cases where both races occupied the same project, buildings were segregated by race.

The first project of the Public Works Administration, Techwood Homes in Atlanta, inaugurated in 1935, is a prime example of the application and impact of this discriminatory policy (Rothstein, 2017). Techwood Homes was built on land where a racially diverse community of 1,600 families had long existed, composed of both black and white

> Government policy caused the creation of new slums as the only housing option for black and economically poor people.

families. In order to build the new housing complex, the federal government demolished the structures where those families lived and replaced them with 604 housing units — all of which were reserved exclusively for white people. This government action not only created a segregated community where there had once been an integrated community; it forced displaced families to look for housing in places were black Americans already lived in overcrowded conditions, intensifying racial segregation in Atlanta.

Government policy also caused the creation of new slums as the only housing option for black and economically poor people. The *Housing Handbook*, written by the U.S. Housing Authority as a guide for states, established that the racial nature of communities had to be preserved. This justified segregation in places where it already existed and implemented segregation in places where it did not exist (Rothstein, 2017). The *Handbook* also reinforced the prevalent belief that any movement of black people into communities made up of white people could threaten property values.

Much of the housing produced using funds provided by the Housing Law of 1949 and its subsequent amendments promoted even more segregation. In 1984, according to Rothstein, investigative reporters from the *Dallas Morning News* visited federally funded public housing projects in 47 metropolitan areas of the United States. The reporters found that close to 10 million residents were living in projects that were segregated by race. They also found that in projects where residents were predominantly white, the facilities, amenities, services, and maintenance were superior, compared to those projects where black people lived.

Nowadays, segregationist policies and practices might not be manifested in such an obvious manner. Many are disguised, but they combine and conspire to make it practically impossible for low-income people of color to have access to decent housing. Included among these discriminatory policies and practices are exclusionary zoning, exorbitant pricing of land and housing, the development of gated neighborhoods, and the lack of public investment and private lending in poverty-stricken areas, especially in areas where people of color reside. Likewise, the quality of public infrastructure and government services offered in poverty-stricken areas is usually inferior to that offered in areas where people with greater economic power reside.

Every day, fewer people have access to adequate housing. According to the renowned architect and urban planner Jaime Lerner (2014), the lack of access to housing is one of the main causes of poverty in the United States and one of the country's most pressing issues. In the same vein, Mathew Desmond (2016) from Harvard University, in an ethnographic study conducted in Milwaukee, Wisconsin, found that families had seen their wages come to a standstill and even lowered, while the cost of housing had increased dramatically. Families that were part of this study became more impoverished with each eviction. Desmond stated that, to this day, the majority of low-income families who rent their housing are forced to spend more than half of their household income on rent and utilities and at least one of every four low-income renters must spend more than 70 percent of their household income for housing.

Millions of people in the United States are evicted every year because they cannot pay their rent. They are displaced through eviction notices rendered by the court, or informal evictions occurring on the fringes of the law. In 2013, one of eight tenant families in the United States could not pay their rent; a similar number were sure that they would eventually be evicted (Desmond, 2016).

Renters are not alone in facing the possibility of losing their homes. This can happen to low-income homeowners too. According to Gottesdiener (2013), between 2007 and 2013 ten million North Americans lost their homes due to foreclosures. The Great Recession harmed people of color far more than it hurt white people. African-Americans, Hispanic-Americans, and Asian-Americans experienced, in the words of James Carr and Katrin Anacker (2012, 3), "a catastrophic loss of wealth as a result of the burst of the national house price bubble in 2006 and the ensuing foreclosure crisis that started in early 2007, both of which have had a disproportionate impact on families and communities of color."[4] In Puerto Rico, according to government statistics, 40,136 mortgages were foreclosed in the decade between 2008 and 2018, which likely means that the same number of families lost their homes.

Discriminatory policies, practices, and patterns must be tackled, whether by governmental intervention or by private action, putting an end to them. It is also the responsibility of individuals who believe in racial and economic justice to denounce discrimination and to search for solutions that alleviate the disparity in the provision of adequate and decent housing for people whose income does not enable them to have access to it.

THE BIOETHICS OF COMMUNITY LAND TRUSTS

The policies that affect housing are tied to policies on land use (Clerc, 2016). The different approaches and regulations on real estate determine who benefits (or not) from the use of land, from the opportunities provided by land, and from the wealth that land produces. It is also important to highlight that land-related decisions are influenced by the values and ethical perspectives of those who are making use of the land. If land is considered a common good, an inheritance received from past generations and entrusted into our care for future generations, our actions in using land will be shaped and constrained in accordance with that perspective. Conversely, if we consider land — and whatever is built upon it — to be a marketable good, subject to price speculation and social exclusion, we will act accordingly.

This latter perspective is prevalent throughout the world, despite consequences that have proven detrimental and hurtful for millions of people who lack secure access to land and housing. This is a social problem on a global scale, requiring solutions that take into account both the personal needs of individuals, for whom adequate housing is essential, and the collective needs of the larger community. Such measures must be sensitive to finding this balance, while also having an ethical, axiological focus on creating the conditions for a decent life.

The CLT model, in this regard, is an ethical model that satisfies an individual's need for safe, decent, and affordable housing, even as it takes into consideration the surrounding community. Individual interests are secured through personal ownership of the housing structure. Collective interests are secured through the community's ownership, control, and care of the land on which the homes are built. Ownership and management of the land in a CLT are carried out by a nonprofit organization with a structure of democratic governance that is sensitive to the community's needs. Both the housing structure and the land are placed beyond the reach of market speculation, which ensures that families of moderate-income or low-income, no matter their race or origin, can exercise a right to decent housing. Since the housing continues to be affordable in perpetuity, that right is protected and extended far into the future.

> Finding and sustaining an equitable balance between the individual and the community is at the heart of the CLT.

It is important to mention, for the purpose of this essay, the values that constitute the roots of the CLT model. Davis (2010) has documented the origins and development of the CLT in the United States, a model that emerged in the 1970s from the Civil Rights Movement in the American South and from an earlier seedbed of theoretical ideas, political movements, and social experiments that had accumulated over many decades. Everything began with a different perspective on how land should be owned and used: recognizing the intrinsic value of land as a shared inheritance; rejecting the speculative buying and selling of land; and using land to capture wealth for the common benefit of all residents, not for the exclusive benefit of a few landowners. Homes could rightfully belong to individuals, but land rightfully belonged to the community, which had a shared responsibility to nurture and preserve it for future generations.

This principle of finding and sustaining an equitable balance between the individual and the community is at the heart of bioethics. It is at the heart of the CLT as well. As far back as 1982, in one of the first books written about this new model of tenure, the authors described why a CLT was needed and how it worked in the following way:

> Our present property arrangements are not working well enough. It makes sense to look for alternative approaches that are based on respect for the legitimate interests of both individuals and communities and that provide an effective means of balancing these interests. The community land trust is one such approach (Institute for Community Economics, 1982, 8).

It is also worth emphasizing the democratic and inclusive character of the governance of most CLTs. The model strengthens and empowers community members, allowing them to exert a degree of control over the lands held by the CLT, the structures that are built on these lands, and the stewardship services that are provided for the long-term care of the buildings and the people who occupy them. The organization has a constant presence, since its corporate membership and governance structure are composed of residents from the community it serves. This relationship is also nurtured by engaging a body of informed people in the organization's development decisions and policy making processes.

The CLT model has three intrinsic elements, namely: sustainable community development that is led by an organization accountable to its community; development that is carried out mainly for the purpose of providing housing that will remain affordable in perpetuity for people who are low-income; and development that occurs on community-owned land that the market cannot reach. This mixture of elements enables a place-based community to maintain its physical integrity, to preserve its cultural inheritance, and to protect the land's natural attributes for future generations.

According to Davis (2010), behind and beyond this basic structure — what is sometimes known as the "classic" CLT — there lies great adaptability, allowing organizations to adjust the model according to the needs and preferences of their own community. Notwithstanding such versatility, however, the model is imbued with similar values each time a CLT is established. These values arise from a sense of responsibility to prevent the displacement of vulnerable populations and to fulfill the basic needs of people who have been excluded from the political and economic mainstream. This is not welfare, but personal improvement and collective empowerment, a program that is focused on the development of humans as citizens exercising their rights and their duties.

The CLT that arose on the mainland of the United States has been an inspiration for community organizations in other countries. This includes two very different CLTs that are geographically distant, but rather similar in terms of their purposes. One of these CLTs was organized in San Juan, Puerto Rico and the other in Voi, Kenya.[5] The purpose of both was to formalize and standardize the relationship with land for residents who were living in informal settlements without land titles. Their CLTs gave them security of tenure as individuals, but it also allowed them to take collective control of their own development and the environment surrounding them, preventing the involuntary displacement of low-income people.

The ownership and use of land in the CLT are far from the dominant tradition of treating land as a commodity, subject to market pricing and speculative hoarding. CLT's live and practice a land ethic that is closer to what Aldo Leopold had urged in *A Sand County Almanac* (1949), treating land as an inheritance that is entrusted to our stewardship for

> The common ground of the CLT is
> put to use for the common good.

future generations. The common ground of the CLT is put to use for the common good. Furthermore, when land is placed under the control of an organization that is accountable to a particular community, it can be managed and developed with a sense of permanent care and shared responsibility by people who are caring for something that does not personally belong to them.

This land ethic is combined with the attention that is also owed to the person who will make use of the structure or improvements on the land. According to data provided by the Grounded Solutions Network, covering 2,844 families or individuals living in home-ownership units in 32 CLTs across the United States of America, 63% are occupied by female-headed households (Grounded Solutions Network, 2019).

Two legal entitlements coexist harmoniously within the same form of tenure: the collective entitlement of land under community governance and the individual entitle-ment of the structural improvements, owned and occupied by the person who acquires or builds it. Both contribute to the empowerment of the community that surrounds this property, strengthening the social fabric and creating a foundation for personal well-be-ing and collaboration.

At the same time, this mixed-ownership model of tenure contributes to the creation of environmentally conscious communities that have the ability to manage change and are committed to the sustainable development of their surroundings. This has been the experience of many CLTs, especially the one created by the Caño Martín Peña communi-ties in San Juan, Puerto Rico. The Caño Martín Peña CLT is making possible the Martín Peña Canal Ecosystem Restoration Project, an environmental justice project that will benefit not only the Caño Martín Peña communities, but also the capital city of San Juan. For many years, highly contaminated water from this canal has flooded the impoverished houses of the residents of the adjacent Caño Martín Peña communities. In order to con-trol flooding, the canal had to be dredged. As a consequence, many households needed to be relocated and new infrastructure needed to be built. As the owner and steward of lands along the canal that were formerly owned by the government, the CLT has made them available for the relocation of residents and for the construction of the appropriate infrastructure that will keep the canal's water clean after dredging.

Making land available for such purposes was a conscious and conscientious decision of the CLT and of the residents who live on the CLT's land. It is worth noting that mar-ket-oriented, individual land ownership would have prevented the Caño Martín Peña communities from realizing these benefits: clean water, a dredged canal, and the perma-nence of the communities in an area that people have been calling home for a century (Algoed, Hernández and Rodríguez, 2018).

As important as the contribution of CLTs in terms of the conservation of the envi-ronment, we should also pay attention to what CLT organizations do for the people who benefit from a CLT's sensible management and stewardship of land and other assets.

Applying the four general principles that constitute the framework for bioethics that were introduced at the beginning of this essay — respect for the autonomy of our choices, non-maleficence, beneficence, and distributive justice — we may put in perspective the ethics of the CLT model.

Thus, CLT organizations provide community assets for low-income families and marginalized communities who would otherwise not have had access to such resources and to the benefits they entail. When a low-income family or individual acquires a home from a CLT, their decision is taken voluntarily after a well-informed process about the structure of the CLT model, its purpose of providing lasting affordability and benefits for the community, and the implications of this arrangement for the buyer. The CLT educates and alerts the family or individual about resale restrictions in order to keep homes affordable for future generations of low-income buyers; the governance structure of the CLT that requires community engagement; and the fact that the CLT retains ownership of the land, while the family or individual purchases only the improvement built on the land.

CLT organizations make it possible for low-income families to buy and to enjoy a home without jeopardizing other important necessities. In this sense, the CLT is complying with the principle of non-maleficence. The principle of beneficence is also widely met by the CLT model since it provides an effective way to meet one of the most important and urgent needs of every human being; that is, to attain a home. But CLT organizations go farther, for they are also creating jobs, promoting quality of life, creating energy-efficient homes, and revitalizing neighborhoods (Thaden and Lowe, 2014).

Market-oriented practices have proven to be a failure in meeting the housing needs of low-income and moderate-income families and individuals. In a market environment, there is neither fairness nor equality when a buyer lacks the resources to acquire or sustain a home. Mortgage banks and other financial institutions have a single priority; that is, to make money for their investors. CLT organizations, on their part, have made it possible for poor people to attain and keep decent and quality homes that are within their economic means; and at the same time, the CLT model has helped these families or individuals to build wealth and to enhance their future.

The question that guides a bioethical analysis is the same question that drives us to ask ourselves and to determine, "What is right?" When deliberating over the negative consequences of treating land as a commodity — whether in the provision of housing or in the preservation of farmland — there is no doubt that a CLT, in its ethical management of land, is more likely to produce results that ensure both a right to housing and an opportunity to promote food security. We should give serious consideration to the CLT model. Said reasoning is supported by the fact that, at the moment, the CLT model is helping to alleviate inequity in the provision of adequate and decent housing for thousands of people whose income does not allow them to have access to these resources. This is confirmed by the growing number of CLTs being organized throughout the world, of which the preceding chapters of this monograph provide testimony and bear witness.

Notes

1. Beauchamp and Childress introduced the four principles of respect for autonomy, non-maleficence, beneficence, and justice in *The Principles of Biomedical Ethics* (1979). Currently in its 7th edition, their book heavily influenced the newly emerging fields of biomedical ethics and bioethics.

2. *The International Bill of Human Rights* consists of the *Universal Declaration of Human Rights, the International Covenant on Civil and Political Rights with the two Optional Protocols, and the International Covenant on Economic, Social, and Cultural Rights.*

3. The Caño Martín Peña communities in San Juan, Puerto Rico and the favelas of Brazil, described in previous chapters of this book, are prime examples.

4. See: James H. Carr and Katrin B. Anacker, *Long-Term Social Impacts and Financial Costs of Foreclosure on Families and Communities of Color: A Review of the Literature* (Washington DC: Annie E. Casey Foundation, National Community Reinvestment Coalition, 2012: 3).

5. The CLT in San Juan, Puerto Rico is discussed in Chapter 11 in *On Common Ground: International Perspectives on the Community Land Trust* (Madison, WI: Terra Nostra Press, 2020). The CLT initiative in Voi, Kenya is discussed in Chapter 14 of the same volume.

References

Algoed, L., Hernández, M., and Rodríguez, L. (2018). El fideicomiso de la tierra del Caño Martín Peña Instrumento notable de regularización de suelo en asentamientos informales. *https://www.lincolninst.edu/publications/working-papers/el-fideicomiso-la-tierra-del-cano-martin-pena*

Beauchamp, T.L. and Childress, J.F. (1979). *The Principles of Biomedical Ethics.* New York: Oxford University Press.

Block v. Hirsch (1921). 256 Supreme Court of the United States, 135, 156.

Clerc, V. (2016). "An outcry against informality. The impact of land on the treatment of precarious settlements, as spaces of political competition." Pp. 105–118 in *Rethinking Precarious Neighborhoods.* Paris: AFD.

Constitución de la Nación Argentina (1994, 22 de agosto).

Constitución Española (1948, 29 de diciembre).

Constitución de la República de Ecuador (2008, 20 de octubre).

Davis, J.E. (2006). "Development without displacement: Organizational and operational choices in starting a community land trust." Reprinted in *The Community Land Trust Reader*, J.E. Davis (ed.). Cambridge, Massachusetts: Lincoln Institute of Land Policy (2010: 259–268).

Davis, J.E. (2010). "Origins and evolution of the community land trust in the United States." Pp. 3–47 in *The Community Land Trust Reader*. Cambridge, Massachusetts: Lincoln Institute of Land Policy.

Desmond, M. (2016). *Evicted: Poverty and Profit in the American City*. New York: Crown Publishers.

Farha, L. (2018). *Report of the Special Rapporteur on Adequate Housing as a Component of the Right to an Adequate Standard of Living, and on the Right to Non-discrimination in this Context. https://www.undocs.org/A/73/310/rev.1*

Ferrer, J. J. (2013). "Teoría ética y deliberación bioética." Pp. 41–85 in *Ensayos en Bioética: Una Perspectiva Puertorriqueña*. San Juan, Puerto Rico: Universidad de Puerto Rico.

Ferrer, J. J. (2016). "Bioéticas principalistas." Pp. 91–116 in *Bioética: El Pluralismo de la Fundamentación*. Madrid: R.B. Servicios Editoriales, S.L.

Gottesdeiner, L. (2013). "10 million americans have had their homes taken away by the banks — often at the point of gun." *https://www.alternet.org/2013/08/10-million-americans-foreclosed-neighborhoods-devastated/*

Grounded Solutions Network (2018). HomeKeeper National Data Hub Administrative Data. Obtained through information request on 4/30/2019.

Hernández, D. and Suglia, S. (2016). "Housing as a social determinant of health." *https://healthequity.globalpolicysolutions.org/wp-content/uploads/2016/12/Housing2.pdf*

Housing Act of 1949, Public Law 81–171, 1949.

Institute for Community Economics (1982). *The Community Land Trust Handbook*. Emmaus, Pennsylvania: Rodale Press.

Leopold, A. (1949). "The land ethic." Pp. 237–264 in *A Sand County Almanac*. New York: Oxford University Press, Inc.

Lerner, J. (2014). *Urban Acupuncture*. Washington: Island Press.

Madden, D. and Marcuse, P. (2017). "The residential is political." Pp. 26–30 in *The Right to the City: A Verso Report*. Brooklyn, New York: Verso.

McNaughton, C. (2010). "Housing, homelessness and capabilities." *Housing, Theory and Society*. doi: 10.1080/14036090902764588

Midheme, E., Moulaert, F. (2013). "Pushing back the frontiers of property: Community land trusts and low-income housing in urban Kenya." *Land Use Policy*, 35, 73–84.

Millones de personas viven sin techo o en casas inadecuadas, un asalto a la dignidad y la vida. (2018). *https://news.un.org/es/story/2018/07/1437721*

Newey, S. (2019). "More than 70 million people forced to flee their homes because of war and persecution." *The Telegraph. https://www.telegraph.co.uk/global-health/ climate-and-people/70-million-people-forced-flee-homes-war-persecution/*

Oficina del Comisionado de Instituciones Financieras (2019, marzo). Foreclosure Unit Residential by Institution. h*ttp://www.ocif.pr.gov/DatosEstadisticos/Pages/default.aspx*

Organización de las Naciones Unidas (1948). Declaración universal de derechos humanos. *https://www.un.org/es/documents/udhr/UDHR_booklet_SP_web.pdf*

Organización de las Naciones Unidas (2015). Objetivos de desarrollo sostenible. Nueva agenda urbana. *https://www.un.org/sustainabledevelopment/es/cities/*

Organización de las Naciones Unidas (2017). Nueva agenda urbana. Conferencia de las Naciones Unidas sobre la Vivienda y el Desarrollo Urbano Sostenible (Hábitat III). *http://habitat3.org/wp-content/uploads/NUA-Spanish.pdf*

Potter, V. (1971). *Bioethics: Bridge to the Future.* New Jersey: Prentice-Hall, Inc.

Rothstein, R. (2017). *The Color of Law: A Forgotten History of How our Government Segregated America.* New York: Liveright Publishing Corporation.

Seoane, J. A. (2016). Argumentación jurídica y bioética. Examen teórico del modelo deliberativo de Diego Gracia. Anuario de Filosofía del Derecho, XXXII, 489–510.

Swann, Robert, Shimon Gottschalk, Erick Hansch, and Edward Webster (1972). *The Community Land Trust: A Guide to a New Model for Land Tenure in America.* Cambridge, Massachusetts: Center for Community Economic Development.

Thaden, E., and Lowe, J. (2014), "Resident and community engagement in community land trusts." *https://www.lincolninst.edu/sites/default/files/pubfiles/2429_1774_thaden_ wp14et1.pdf*

United Nations High Commissioner for Refugees (2019), *Climate Change and Disaster Displacement,* accessed August 27, 2019 from *https://www.unhcr.org/climate-change- and-disasters.html*

5.

Preserving Urban Generativity
The Role of Porous Spaces
in CLT Projects

Verena Lenna

In the last thirty years—at the very least—the urban condition has been described as increasingly segregated and enclaved (Blakely and Snyder, 1997; Soja, 2000; Low, 2001). Cities are the places where the war among corporations happens in the form of the enforcement of existing regulations and the construction of perimeters of consumption. The loss of urbanity is the result of processes of privatisation, dispossession, and expulsion (Sassen, 2014; 2015). Privatisation, by appropriating urban land, takes away from most citizens the right of access and use, resulting in a loss of urbanity. Privatisation of land also takes away the right to *decide* its use, since the property is in private hands. This is often the case with privately owned public spaces as well.[1] Despite conditions imposed by a municipality when approving new developments, requiring ongoing public access to a plaza or courtyard, these spaces can perform in rather exclusive terms because of poor design choices and the scarce involvement of the local community (Schmidt, Nemeth, and Botsford, 2011). This is also true for many buildings acquired by foreign corporations and wealthy investors that are removed from any use by a local community. They stand vacant, occupied only part of the year or waiting for some form of renovation.[2]

On the other hand, spontaneous occupations and the establishment of temporary uses by local communities have frequently shown the variety of needs that abandoned buildings and spaces could respond to, both at an individual and at a collective level. The claim of the right to the city in recent years has produced a city of rights. The multiplication of citizens' initiatives demonstrates the unexhausted creativity of local communities when taking care and making use of available resources, inventing new ways of governing them, while mobilising a wide range of resources and capabilities often unknown to public officials or incompatible with their policies (Ferguson and Urban Drift Projects, 2014). In many cases, practices that have informally emerged around the need to share

Community land trusts can be considered laboratories where urban generativity is fostered.

and to manage a common pool of resources have been so successful as to trigger the interest and the support of municipal governments.[3]

Because of an exclusive approach to the use of resources, what is being lost is not only urban land and the right of concerned communities to decide about its development and use. Also lost is the possibility of spontaneous encounters among actors and communities, interacting with one another and sharing their needs and capabilities. Such encounters enable actors and communities to develop reciprocities, to react to oppressive conditions where necessary, and to generate innovative approaches and answers to emerging needs.

This capability of cities to continuously produce new resources, as a result of the diversity and complexity of the urban milieu, can be called *urban generativity*. As this chapter will try to show, community land trusts can prevent the loss of this capability. They can be considered laboratories where urban generativity is fostered.

URBAN GENERATIVITY AS
THE COMMON WEALTH OF CITIES

The concept of generativity was first suggested by Edmund Husserl, mostly in the 1930s, to describe the transformational nature of the process of becoming, generation after generation, based on pre-existing elements and materials, rather than happening as an unconditioned creation started from scratch.[4] Applied to cities, generativity could effectively explain their resourcefulness and resiliency. As their histories show, cities are adaptive organisations. They have an inherent ability to continuously generate the resources they need in order to transform and to tackle the socio-spatial challenges that emerge over time, expected or unexpected. This is made possible by the accumulation of material and immaterial resources and by forms of knowledge and expertise that are constantly attracted by a city: what Hardt and Negri have called the "common wealth" (Hardt and Negri, 2009).

Such resourcefulness is also currently being theorised by the rising discourse on the "commons." While some scholars regard the city as a whole as being a commons (Salzano, 2009; Marella, 2012; Stavrides, 2016), others prefer to refer to the "urban commons," pointing at the specificity of some forms of commons generated in an urban context. In both cases, what is implied is a generative process of commoning. Among countless definitions and conceptualisations of the commons, the one elaborated by Massimo De Angelis and Stavros Stavrides (AnArchitektur, 2010) highlights precisely such a process:

Commons are not simply resources we share—conceptualizing the commons involves three things at the same time. First, all commons involve some sort of common pool of resources, understood as non-commodified means of fulfilling people's needs. Second, the commons are necessarily created and sustained by communities. . . . Communities are sets of commoners who share these resources and who define for themselves the rules according to which they are accessed and used. . . . In addition to these two elements—the pool of resources and the set of communities—the third and most important element in terms of conceptualizing the commons is the verb "to common"—the social process that creates and reproduces the commons.

The common wealth of cities is their latent ability to generate innovations and solutions by recycling and reinventing existing resources, both material and immaterial. Intuitively, the more that individuals and collectives, citizens and actors are able to interact and to interweave, the larger becomes the field of possibilities, capabilities, and expertise from which new resources and innovative approaches can emerge, meeting a variety of needs. Urban generativity is about the abundance that derives from the opportunity for continuous cooperation and exchange, compensating for the scarcity of many resources, real or artificial; resisting, thereby, the narrow vision of the world that scarcity brings, along with the related risks of both individualism and *désaffiliation,* as Castel has pointed out (Castel and Haroche, 2001). This capability is of the utmost importance to counterbalance the growing privatisation of resources and the shrinking capacities of welfare states, for it operates by disrupting the enclaving, exclusionary trends in the management of resources.

> A common wealth is fuelled by creating the conditions for the interaction of different actors and their expertise.

Urban generativity depends on conditions that allow existing resources and expertise to circulate, combine, disassemble, recombine, and transform according to the contexts and the specific needs of the concerned communities. Urban generativity is impeded by policies and forms of appropriation that define exclusive and homogeneous realms of interactions and governance; and by the imposition of externally conceived, a priori forms of governance that are incapable of being site-responsive. By contrast, a common wealth is fuelled and valorized by creating the conditions for the interaction of different actors and their expertise. The model of the CLT suggests a viable approach in that direction.

SPACE MATTERS

The model of the CLT is founded on the recognition of a *bundle of rights.*[5] The rights are those possessed by specific groups of users, inhabitants, owners, and managers of land and buildings who co-create the rules and share the responsibilities concerning a given CLT's project. Their equitable and sustainable allocation should enable a CLT to fulfil its main purpose: the preservation of the land and its development for the common good.

Rights, rules and responsibilities are necessarily defined by the context and the conditions under which a given project is supposed to be established. There is no recipe, however, for ensuring the coexistence and compatibility of those rights in the framework of a given project, including the right of the community to have access to the land and to the built assets in the long run, the right to homeownership of individual households, the right of local actors to have a voice concerning the potential transformations of their neighbourhood, and the right of public agencies to decide about assets that could benefit the city as a whole. Which form should the allocation of these rights take? How many square meters of space should be occupied by each household? How should access to the shared spaces be organised? How should the inhabitants get involved in the maintenance of the building? It is through the concrete uses made possible by a specific project that those rights will be expressed and substantiated. On the one hand, the recognition of those rights is the *sine qua non* for establishing a CLT project; on the other hand, the bundle of uses is what allows the residents of a CLT project to practice them and to verify their compatibility and related responsibilities.

Above all, coming to terms with the *space* in a particular project is what allows a given bundle of rights to exist. The morphologic qualities of a site and a building provide the

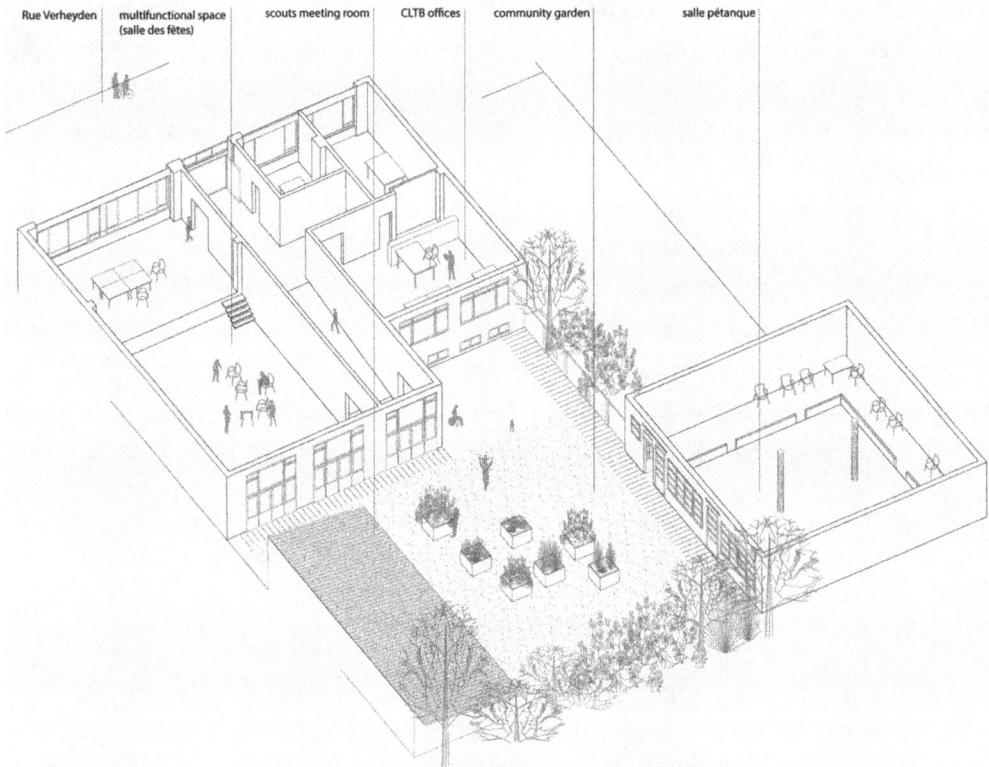

Fig. 5.1. Diagram depicting the spaces and activities interweaving at the ground floor of 121 Rue Verheyden, during the initial occupation of the site. VERENA LENNA

form and envelope for specific uses, pushing the concerned actors and users to work together not only so they can coexist, but also —and most importantly — so the project's resources can be preserved (Lenna, 2019). The CLT projects being realised in Brussels are good examples. They show how space can contribute to the interweaving of individuals and collectives, and the related rights and uses, thus increasing their sustainability.

Le Nid ("the nest") is one of the first projects developed by the Brussels CLT (CLTB). The property once belonged to the Catholic Parish. This helps to explain the spatial characteristics of the main building and of the site as a whole (see Fig. 25.1). Before renovation, a green metallic door and a generous entrance gave access to a large ramp into the ground-floor corridor, sloping directly into the *interieur d'îlot*. On the right of the entrance, there was a huge *salle des fêtes*. This hall was used by CLTB, during the long period between acquiring the building and beginning its rehabilitation and conversion to permanent housing, to organise meetings, assemblies and other activities, including those of other local associations. On the left side of the entrance, a cafeteria served as office space for the small CLTB team. At the second and third floor, each room was occupied by tenants whose rents were set to cover only basic expenses.

The ramp from the front door provided a direct connection from the public dimension of the street to the semi-hidden, collective space of the courtyard. Located in the courtyard, there was a small white construction normally used by local groups of scouts and a *salle pétanque*. A few chairs and a small table allowed the building's occupants to enjoy the sun during lunch breaks or any other occasions. The courtyard was occupied by plant containers and by a small, makeshift greenhouse for gardening activities involving neighbours and other users of the building. Outside of working hours for CLTB's staff,

Fig. 5.2. Interior courtyard at 121 Rue Verheyden. VERENA LENNA

the courtyard was used mostly for convivial activities, allowing future inhabitants and present users to gather, to meet their neighbours, and to expand their network of social relations.

Such a variety of activities was orchestrated by CLTB's staff and board as part of giving life to a new organisation and for creating some relational premises for Le Nid to be established on sustainable terms. They were possible because of the peculiar morphology of the plot and of the building, a factor that subsequently would play a crucial role in realising Le Nid. Mainly conceived as a residential project for seven households, Le Nid was also planned from the very beginning to host a community garden, to offer shared spaces for the inhabitants, and to provide a multi-functional building for both the inhabitants and the neighbourhood, once the *salle pétanque* was renovated.

The interweaving of different uses is a characteristic not only of Le Nid, but of most of CLTB's projects. It implies the pragmatic involvement of other local actors — beyond the households who will occupy the housing — in planning, designing, and utilizing the space in a given project. Such involvement is both a product and pre-condition of CLTB's tripartite structure of governance and CLTB's commitment to participatory decision making. At the same time, the combination of functions and the ensuing convergence of actors are intended to promote the integration of both the project and its inhabitants in the neighbourhood. The result thus is twofold. In a virtuous circle, not only would the neighbourhood's liveliness be improved, but also the CLTB project would be better maintained, a result of the interest and involvement of different users, contributing according to their specific forms of expertise and availability.[6]

Therefore, in the specific case of Le Nid, accessibility to a common pool of resources — the courtyard, the former *salle pétanque*, the shared spaces — was planned not only to fulfill the needs and rights of different communities of users. It was also intended to enable these communities to take care of their common resources and to assume their responsibilities, so that those uses could be maintained in the long run for the common good of present and future generations. For this to happen, as noted already, a project's spatial conditions are crucial to fostering exchange and encounter among the newly arrived households, users of the site, and the pre-existing urban fabric. It is also for this reason that the CLTB has implemented an intensive participatory process, mostly focusing on spatial issues.

By designing the articulation of space at Le Nid and in its other projects, CLTB has the purpose of creating the conditions for a sustainable coexistence of the different activities and of the needs of the inhabitants and other users. As a result, a good living environment can be maintained, both on a relational level and in terms of preservation of the built assets. Motivated by individual needs and pushed by the challenge to collectively manage what will become their shared resources, households and local actors are called to imagine, through a series of *ateliers* and other meetings, what their future homes will look like and how their life together might be. They are asked to envision and to plan the activities they would like to organise and might be able to maintain according to their concrete possibility to engage. This exercise not only leads to the elaboration of a number of suggestions concerning the design of the space, a *cahier des recommandations* for those architects interested in proposing a project; it also encourages examination of the distribution of responsibilities. What should the function of the common spaces be? Which activities could be imagined in the former *salle pétanque,* compatible with the everyday lives of the households? Who will take care of the community garden? What access to the courtyard should be allowed during the weekend?

Space determines the possibilities for interacting and collaborating to preserve a common pool of resources.

Space matters. The morphological characteristics of a building or of an urban block play a crucial role, either impeding or facilitating the encounter and the collaboration of the concerned communities. It is by coming to terms with the specific spatial potentials and limitations of a given site or building that inhabitants and users become aware of their actual possibilities, necessarily reconsidering their own plans and needs so that those of others can also be realised. In that way, individual rights and needs are fulfilled as part of a larger collective endeavour, overcoming individualism in the name of the common good. It is by confronting the actual characteristics of space that inhabitants and users can learn about their actual capacities to manage their living environment, to engage, and to assume responsibilities.[7] Shaped by design preferences, space determines the conditions under which different users will practice their rights; space determines the possibilities for interacting and collaborating around the shared responsibility to preserve a common pool of resources.

CLT PROJECTS AS LABORATORIES OF URBAN GENERATIVITY

What can be learned from the Brussels CLT is that an inclusive approach to expanding and protecting land-based resources, founded on the collaboration of different concerned actors and inhabitants — a hallmark of the CLT model — seems to be made easier and more consistent when a project creates the spatial conditions for cooperation to happen. Like a sponge allowing water to leak in and to enter every available cavity, the morphology of the building and the site at Le Nid allows different users to access the internal courtyard, the *salle pétanque,* and the housing units. Such a spatial configuration, which could be described as "porous," can be found in many of CLTB's projects, though with variations determined by the characteristics of a given site and by the specific choices made by the future users during the design process. Delimitations and openings, corridors and

> The porous perimeters of a CLT's projects provide the physical and relational conditions to revive the existing urban fabric.

thresholds, shared spaces: they allow the rights of different concerned communities to be fulfilled and their resources to be protected. Inappropriate uses are impeded, while the inclusive attitude of CLT model is maintained. Accessibility is regulated by collectively conceived design choices and rules. They make possible the interweaving of private, collective and semi-public activities, thus realising the bundle of rights that CLTs recognise and allocate.

The concept of porosity has been used by urbanists Bernardo Secchi and Paola Viganò to depict urban spaces that are designed to pay attention "to practices, changes, fractures in space, urban materials and availability, possibilities for new flows" (Viganò, 2009). A porous spatial configuration, such as that found at Le Nid, reinforces an inclusive, collaborative approach to the management of property and spatial resources, based on the CLT's unique allocation of rights. By making room for different users and their needs, a porous space, almost by definition, has a potential for triggering socio-spatial experimentation. It is a space of encounter and reciprocal adjustment, where the coexistence of different activities and communities can be tested, so that their different rights can be practiced. It is a space where different forms of expertise and the capabilities of the concerned actors, challenged by the need to oversee and to care for a common pool of resources, can combine and complement each other, leading eventually to required solutions and innovations.

Additionally, a porous space is a space where site-responsivity can be built. All CLT projects have in common the same basic approach to property rights and governance, but each project is quite site-specific: that is, each has a unique combination of inhabitants and local users with different needs and expectations, along with different socio-spatial conditions within a given context and moment in time. Each project, therefore, to be realised and maintained in the long run will have to conceive and to implement *ad hoc* solutions and forms of collaboration, creating occasions of exchange with the pre-existing urban fabric and taking into account the potentials and limitations of the specific piece of urban ecology that will support it. The porous perimeters of a CLT's projects provide the physical and relational conditions for future inhabitants, users, local actors and administrators to encounter and to create a new piece of the city or to revive the existing urban fabric, based on their capacity to contribute, realising what Castel and Haroche would call their *stratégies de vie* (Castel and Haroche, 2001).

By embedding themselves in a given section of the city, these projects necessarily have the capacity to transform it. This means that by being inclusive and porous, CLT projects not only have an *introverted* dimension, concerning the adjacent, directly interested inhabitants and users; they have an *extroverted* dimension as well, involving the neighbours and other local actors. They allow not only specific solutions and spontaneous forms of reciprocity to emerge, but also to become the starting point for further innovations. Other contexts and other actors are benefited beyond the boundaries of the specific projects that engendered them and beyond the immediate concerns of developing and maintaining a newly constructed or rehabilitated residential building or urban block.

What the CLT model seems to suggest is that inclusion is not only about a passive coexistence of uses and users; that is, who will have gained access to a space or resource. It is not only about simply accepting or integrating the newly arrived. Inclusion is, first and foremost, about the possibility of contributing. It is about the incommensurable, generative potential of diversity, combining and recombining different perspectives, expertise and approaches; completing each other's availability and capabilities. Out of these assemblages comes the hybridisation of forms of knowledge and innovative strategies, resources, and answers to the emerging needs of cities. These forms are sustainable because they are being proposed by a range and variety of concerned communities. From a design perspective, spatial porosity is an element that can promote urban generativity: because after having absorbed, a sponge necessarily releases its liquids.

——

CONCLUSION

Community land trusts are known for holding land and developing it for the common good. However, another major capability of CLTs—less recognized or emphasised—is that of fuelling urban generativity. A form of property and of governance that entails the convergence of a variety of actors and communities, with the purpose of co-creating the rules and sharing the responsibilities for site-specific projects, can trigger urban generativity, thus engendering a common pool of new resources and innovative approaches for meeting the emerging needs of cities. The projects developed by the CLT in Brussels show that such a capability is fuelled not only by an inclusive system of decision-making. The spontaneous interweaving and cooperation of individuals and collectives are also fostered by porous spatial configurations, especially when resources are collectively used and governed.

CLTs interject inclusive forms of governance and rights of property into an urban social-spatial grid that is otherwise becoming more and more exclusive. Functioning as urban laboratories, through their porous delimitations, a CLT's projects pour out experiments in governance, new forms of reciprocities and collaboration, and institutional innovations and arrangements that can potentially address a variety of issues, benefiting the city as a whole. Through their *modus operandi*, what these projects suggest is that urban generativity, as a vital common wealth of cities, can only exist through inclusion.

Notes

1. "Privately owned public spaces, also known by the acronym POPS, are spaces dedicated to public use and enjoyment and which are owned and maintained by private property owners, in exchange for bonus floor area or waivers." Source: *https://www1.nyc.gov/ site/planning/plans/pops/pops.page*

2. This was reported by some of the local actors I interviewed, concerning the situation in the Brussels Capital Region. The same is happening in many other cities in Europe, Great Britain, and North America, where residential (and commercial) buildings are being used by foreign investors for "wealth storage," instead of being renovated and made available for use by residents of local communities. See, for example: *https://inequality. org/wp-content/uploads/2018/09/Towering-Excess-Report-Final.pdf*

3. Examples can be found in cities such as Barcelona, Ghent, Lille and in many others in Italy, where a sort of protocol has been established to help local governments to develop commons-oriented policies for the management of shared resources (*https://www. labsus.org/*). Some scholars, however, have questioned the actual contribution an urban landscape that is fragmented by one thousand alternatives could bring to the making of a democratic scenario, with the risk of losing sight of the need for more structural efforts (Armony, 2004; Bianchetti, 2016).

4. According to Steinbock (1995), "For Husserl, generativity is both the process of becoming, hence the process of 'generation,' and a process that occurs over the 'generations,' hence specifically the process of historical and social movement."

5. The "bundle of rights" is a metaphor to explain the coexistence of different rights and responsibilities concerning the use, access, and temporary or permanent possession of real estate. Especially in Common Law countries, it is employed to describe property ownership as a collection of different rights.

6. At the start of a project, the CLTB has the main responsibility for guiding the inhabitants and future users in how to maintain the project. Over time, however, the inhabitants should assume increasing responsibility for their own project, converging around the need to govern and to manage their common living environment. The stewardship role that is played by the CLTB is about teaching and guidance as much as it is about direct responsibility for overseeing a specific project.

7. The whole participatory process, even when not focusing on spatial matters, provides the occasion for the inhabitants and future users of the project to voice their needs and desires concerning their future living environment. Spatial issues and choices however have the power of guiding imagination towards plausible everyday-life scenarios.

References

AnArchitektur. 2010. "On the Commons: A Public Interview with Massimo De Angelis and Stavros Stavrides." *E-Flux Journal*, no. 17.

Armony, Ariel. 2004. *The Dubious Link. Civic Engagement and Democratisation*. Stanford: Stanford University Press.

Bianchetti, Cristina. 2016. *Spazi Che Contano. Il Progetto Urbanistico in Epoca Neo-Liberale*. Roma: Donzelli.

Blakely, Edward J. and Mary Gail Snyder. 1997. *Fortress America: Gated Communities in the United States*. Cambridge, Massachusetts: Lincoln Institute of Land Policy.

Castel, Robert and Claudine Haroche. 2001. *Propriété Privée, Propriété Sociale, Propriété de Soi: Entretiens Sur La Construction de l'individu Moderne*. Paris: Fayard.

Ferguson, Francesca, and Urban Drift Projects. 2014. *Make Shift City. Renegotiating the Urban Commons*. Berlin: Jovis.

Hardt, Michael and Antonio Negri. 2009. *Common Wealth*. Cambridge, Massachusetts: The Belknap Press of Harvard University Press.

Lenna, Verena. 2019. "The Project of Property as Emancipation: A Community Land Trust in Brussels." Ph.D. Dissertation. Università IUAV di Venezia and Katholieke Universiteit Leuven.

Low, Setha. 2001. "The Edge and the Center: Gated Communities and the Discourse of Urban Fear." *American Anthropologist* 103 (1).

Marella, Maria Rosaria, ed. 2012. *Oltre Il Pubblico e Il Privato. Per Un Diritto Dei Beni Comuni*. Verona: Ombre Corte.

Salzano, Edoardo. 2009. *La Città Come Bene Comune*. Bologna: Ogni Uomo è Tutti Gli Uomini.

Sassen, Saskia. 2014. *Expulsions. Brutality and Complexity in the Global Economy*. Cambridge, Massachusetts: The Belknap Press of Harvard University Press.

————. 2015. "Who Owns Our Cities — and Why This Urban Takeover Should Concern Us All." *The Guardian*, 2015. *https://www.theguardian.com/cities/2015/nov/24/who-owns-our-cities-and-why-this-urban-takeover-should-concern-us-all*.

Schmidt, Stephan, Jeremy Nemeth and Erik Botsford. 2011. "The Evolution of Privately Owned Public Spaces in New York City." *Urban Design International*, 270–84.

Soja, Edward W. 2000. *Postmetropolis: Critical Studies of Cities and Regions.* New York: Wiley.

Stavrides, Stavros. 2016. *The City as a Commons.* London: Zed Books.

Steinbock, Anthony J. 1995. *Home and Beyond: Generative Phenomenology after Husserl.* Evanston, Illinois: Northwestern University Press.

Viganò, Paola. 2009. "The Metropolis of the Twenty-First Century: The Project of a Porous City." *Oase* 80 (On territories).

6.

Better Together
The Challenging, Transformative Complexity
of Community, Land, and Trust

John Emmeus Davis

There is nothing simple about the community land trust. It is a complicated construct with many moving parts, all of which must work in concert for the CLT's unique approach to community-led development of permanently affordable housing on community-owned land to be done well. Its complexity is compounded by the fact that not every CLT is the same. The model's design is being continuously reinvented, giving rise to numerous organizational and operational variations.[1] These refinements have been crucial to the CLT's proliferation, helping it to adapt to a wide range of local conditions in a dozen different countries and to find acceptance among populations with diverse social, political, and economic interests.

The CLT's organizational and operational complexity is not merely a matter of the multiplicity and mutability of its constituent elements, however. The biggest challenge in mastering the model and making it sing lies in understanding that the whole is greater than the sum of its parts. It is the combination of community, land, and trust that contributes the most to a CLT's performance. The dynamic interaction of its three main components is what enables an organization to be a CLT and to behave like one.

Describing this complexity to people who are hearing about the CLT for the first time has never been easy. The most common technique employed by instructors like me has been to picture the CLT as a Venn diagram, where the model's principal components and essential concerns are depicted as three intersecting circles. "Community" is described in terms of a CLT's distinctive approach to involving residents of its chosen service area in guiding and governing the organization. "Land" is described in terms of the organization's distinctive approach to holding land forever, acreage that is scattered throughout a CLT's service area and conveyed via long-term ground leases to the owners of residential or commercial buildings. "Trust" is described in terms of a CLT's distinctive approach to the long-term stewardship of lands and buildings entrusted into its care, an operational

COMMUNITY
(Organization)

LAND
(Ownership)

TRUST
(Operation)

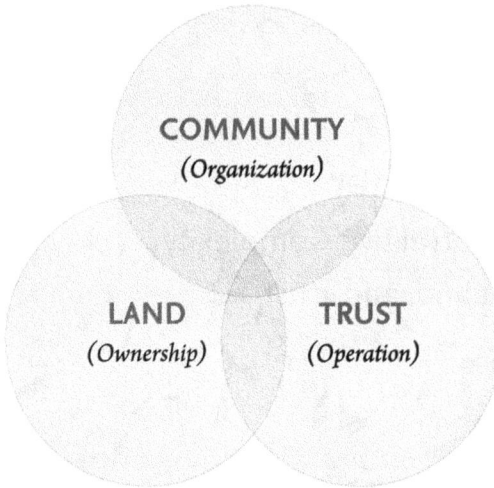

Fig. 6.1. Venn diagram depicting the "classic" community land trust.

priority that plays out in the programs of most CLTs through policies and procedures designed to preserve the affordability, quality, and security of heavily subsidized, privately owned housing.

This three-ring schematic has the advantage of simplicity. It allows a complicated model to be readily grasped in its entirety and then directs attention toward each component, inviting a closer examination of the key features and common variations that constitute the CLT's unusual treatment of organization, ownership, and operation. But simplicity can also have negative, unintended consequences. Indeed, I have come to suspect that our go-to image for illustrating and discussing what is widely known in the United States as the "classic" CLT may be inadequate at best and harmful at worst. It obscures too many of the complex interactions that invigorate the model. It overlooks too often the transformative potential of such complexity, as a CLT goes about its virtuous business of rebuilding a place of residence by restructuring the twin pillars of property and power.

Simplification is not only a problem for pedagogy but for practice as well. How a CLT is depicted has an effect on how it is implemented. Our attempt to cope with the model's messiness by stuffing it into three tidy circles on a static diagram means that we spend most of our time investigating the contents of each circle, while frequently failing to relate one circle to another. When that happens, when the interactions among the model's components are overlooked, we accidentally suggest that any one of them may be safely removed without damaging the whole. After all, if organization, ownership, and operation can be separately examined, they can be separately implemented — perhaps even discarded. Or so it would seem.

This occurs with distressing frequency in everyday practice. For example, a city government or non-governmental organization (NGO) may endorse a CLT's operational commitment to the lasting affordability of publicly subsidized, privately owned housing, while also embracing ground leasing as the most effective strategy for implementing and administering a stewardship regime. But the prospect of including a neighborhood's residents in planning a CLT's projects, in shaping its policies, and participating in its governance is considered an arduous, time-consuming annoyance. So this troublesome component is deleted from the start — or diluted along the way.

Another frequent occurrence: an NGO may behave like a CLT organizationally and operationally, engaging local residents in the guidance and governance of its activities while also providing a full complement of stewardship services, but the organization's leaders or funders decide to dispense with community ownership of the underlying land. Developing and financing affordable housing on leased land is deemed too difficult to do, so the CLT's bedrock commitment to owning land on behalf of a place-based community — and never reselling it — is set aside.[2]

This propensity for pruning cannot be attributed solely to the imagery that is commonly used in introducing the CLT. But when practitioners or funders who profess to support community land trusts do not hesitate in removing one or two of the model's main components for the sake of convenience, sawing off branches that have historically defined the CLT, it is fair to ask whether some of the blame for bestowing a license to lop should be assigned to the manner in which the model is described.

Perhaps the moment has come to find a different image to illustrate the CLT. If so, one option might be to substitute the dynamic mobile of Mr. Calder for the static diagram of Mr. Venn. I've been wondering of late whether it might be helpful, in other words, to portray the CLT as something akin to one of Alexander Calder's kinetic creations: a suspended apparatus that is finely balanced to turn freely in the breeze while remaining stably in place. *Community* would constitute one of the cross-pieces from which a variety of organizational configurations were hung. *Land* would be the second, balancing various interests of ownership. *Trust* would be the third, an operational strut to which were attached the multi-colored duties of stewardship, each festooned with weights and counter-weights all their own.

The best thing about this whimsical image of the CLT-as-mobile is that it cautions against the reckless removal of any component, lest the whole construct collapses. It also accepts as ordinary the real-world tensions that are intrinsic to community development. The artistry inherent in the construction of a mobile, like the artistry inherent in designing, constructing, and managing a CLT, lies in making a virtue out of necessity. Rather than pretending that interests are not in competition (and sometimes in conflict), the tensions that exist among various groups who share the same territory become the raw material for a creative endeavor that has as its greatest challenge and highest accomplishment a mastery of balance.[3]

A friend of Alexander Calder's, Saul Steinberg, once said of Calder that he was "a particular American type: the dogged tinker. We saw in him the face of a man who is always working on a perpetual motion machine, which he then sends to the patent office."[4] Mirrored in the image of the CLT-as-mobile, we find the faces of inventive practitioners engaged in a similar project. They are dogged tinkerers all, even if many of them are not American, as the model spreads to other countries. They are artistic realists who accept the challenge of finding the practical fulcrum at every point in a CLT's design. By their hands, the weighty concerns of "community," "land," and "trust" are adapted to the windy conditions within their own communities and kept stably, durably in balance.

Such a balancing act doesn't happen by itself. The CLT is a rather elegant model of community development, displaying a remarkable degree of adaptability and resiliency across a range of conditions, but it depends upon talented people to put it in place and to keep it aloft. Agency is as important as structure in fashioning and maintaining this perpetual motion machine. There are artists behind the art.

Much as I like this metaphor for describing how a CLT is built and behaves, however, I'm not quite ready to abandon the three-ring diagram that has long been used in trainings to depict the "classic" CLT. Yes, that familiar schematic has made it harder to appreciate the carefully balanced complexity of the model as a whole. Yes, it has made it easier to prune the model beyond recognition. But the fault lies less in Mr. Venn than in ourselves. Instead of substituting one metaphor for another, a more reasonable course of action would be for us to make better use of the imagery already in hand.

> More than the model's reinvention of each component, it is their combination that gives vitality, resilience, and power to a CLT.

We are not mistaken in picturing the CLT as a trio of interlocking circles; nor are we misguided in taking the time to understand, separately and thoroughly, the internal workings of the model's main components. Where we go wrong, I believe, is devoting too little attention to the spaces where the circles overlap. As a result, we tend to overlook the dynamic interaction of organization, ownership, and operation — and the delicate balance that must exist among them for a CLT to prosper.

These interactions are seldom discussed, rarely studied, and poorly understood. Such neglect is a major blunder, because the synergies produced by these interactions are what enable a CLT to perform to its highest potential. Organization and operation are made more effective by the innovative way in which a CLT's property is owned. The ownership and operation of a CLT's property are made more effective by the innovative way in which a CLT is organized. Ownership and organization are made more effective by the innovative way in which a CLT's lands and buildings are operated. More than the model's reinvention of each component, it is their combination that gives vitality, resilience, and power to a CLT.

Why go to all the trouble of identifying these interactions? What advantages would advocates and practitioners derive from a deeper understanding of the mutually reinforcing relationships among a CLT's main components? To my mind, they would possess a new set of tools for making their case. They would have at their fingertips a more compelling rationale for upholding the integrity of the CLT, which might stiffen their resolve in resisting the model's dismemberment. They would also have in hand a more robust measure for evaluating the model's performance, gauging when a CLT is working well and when it is not; providing them, too, with a finely calibrated scale for weighing whether a proposed adjustment to one of the model's main components is likely to preserve — or disrupt — the balance on which a CLT depends.

A few additional remarks about this balancing act. The particular genius of practitioners who are charged with implementing this unusual model of tenure, as suggested earlier, is their artistry in managing property-based interests that often compete — and sometimes conflict. CLT practitioners neither wish away these pesky tensions, nor regard their persistence as a sign of failure. They fashion them into something equitably in synch and sustainably in balance. Within the CLT's two-party structure of ownership, the ground lease is designed to balance the competing interests of the nonprofit landowner and those of the owners of any buildings located on the nonprofit's lands. Within the CLT's organizational structure, the two-part membership and three-part board are designed to balance the competing interests of the people who live on the nonprofit's lands and the neighbors who live around them. Within the model's operational structure, a CLT's stewardship regime is designed to balance competing priorities of enabling low-income households to gain access to homeownership and to build wealth in the present versus preserving that same homeownership opportunity for lower-income households in the future.

These difficult and daunting acts of balance are on daily display within the three-ring circus of a CLT. They capture our attention and win our applause. But we often fail to notice the other high-wire acts of derring-do that are being performed with quiet aplomb where the rings overlap. Here, too, CLT practitioners must skillfully balance competing interests and concerns.

There is an inherent tension, for instance, between the roles of CLT-as-developer and CLT-as-organizer. A CLT that tilts too heavily toward the former, giving too little weight to building a base of support within its service area, is unlikely to have the political clout to compete for land and money from its local government. It is unlikely to possess the legitimacy and loyalty that enables an organization like a CLT to surmount not-in-my-backyard opposition to its projects and to build local support for its unfamiliar form of tenure. Conversely, a CLT that tilts too heavily the other way, giving too much weight to every objection that might be raised by a vocal minority within its own service area or within its own membership, is likely to stumble in striving to acquire land, to assemble capital, and to develop affordable housing. Every CLT is forced to find a point of equilibrium, in other words, between building a substantial portfolio and cultivating an engaged constituency, maintaining a delicate balance between ownership and organization.

Another example. A community land trust that becomes too heavy-handed in carrying out its operational duties of stewardship can steadily undermine the "marriage of convenience" that must be maintained with the individuals and organizations that use its land. An imbalance in this pivotal relationship can increase the organization's costs, requiring constant intervention by the CLT to ensure that homes on its land are kept affordable, that buildings are kept in good repair, and that mortgages are paid. Conversely, a CLT that operates with too little oversight runs the risk of failing to fulfill its operational commitment to preserving the affordability, condition, and security of housing and other buildings entrusted into its care. There is a delicate balance between operation and organization.

Performing these feats of balance will always be a challenge. But the odds of success are greatly improved when practitioners appreciate on a deeper level the many interactions among a CLT's main components. There is a certain irony here. At the same time that practitioners are handed a stronger rationale for upholding the integrity of the "classic" CLT, they are allowed a wider latitude in modifying that model as needed. They are able to weigh with greater precision any proposed adjustments, watching closely to make sure their well-intentioned tinkering with the internal workings of organization, ownership, or operation does not throw their carefully designed construct completely out of whack. Practitioners who come to appreciate the model's interactive complexity discover that their license to lop has been revoked, but their freedom to improvise has been expanded.

> The transformative potential of a CLT is greatest when every part of this complex composition is present and performed in harmony with the others.

A deeper appreciation for the power of complexity also puts practitioners in the best position to bend the trajectory of local development toward justice. That is not to say that programs or policies that embrace less than the full package of the "classic" CLT are without merit. By itself, a community's ownership of land provides a platform for protecting access to goods, services, and homes for lower-income residents who might otherwise be extruded or excluded from a neighborhood. By itself, an organization's commitment to giving residents a voice in guiding development in their own locale and a role in governing the organization doing that development are marked improvements over top-down approaches to neighborhood revitalization. By itself, an operational commitment to the lasting affordability of housing, secured through a watchful stewardship regime, is a vast improvement over policies and programs that allow affordably priced homes produced through public dollars or private donations to leak away. Each reinvention of organization, ownership, and operation has value; each helps to make place-based development more equitable in the short run and more sustainable over time. But two components are better than one, and three are best. The transformative potential of a CLT is greatest when every part of this complex composition is present and performed in harmony with the others.[5]

At the risk of trotting out one metaphor too many, let me end with a story that predates my personal involvement with community land trusts. Nearly fifty years ago, I spent summers in the mountains of southern Appalachia, doing community organizing as a member of a project called the Student Health Coalition.[6] One of my fellow organizers, who was eager to immerse himself in Appalachian culture, managed to persuade a retired coal miner to give him weekly lessons in playing the country fiddle. My friend was a quick study in mastering the instrument's fingering because he already played the guitar. He had a harder time making the fiddle sing, however, as he sawed clumsily across the strings.

Exasperated by his pupil's lack of progress, the gray-haired fiddler would interrupt their sessions again and again with the same admonishment: "Charles, any damn fool can figure out where to put his fingers. The music is in the bow, boy; the music is in the bow."

Faced with the challenge of teaching people to play an instrument as demanding as the CLT, I am frequently reminded of the old fiddler's advice. Whether introducing the model to a new audience or bringing the model to a new venue, the first lessons must always be focused on getting the fingering right within the separate spheres of ownership, organization, and operation. A novice must have a basic command of each component before tackling more difficult exercises. But that will never be enough to coax a compelling tune from a CLT. Any damn fool can figure out where to put his or her fingers, sliding along the taut strings of organization, ownership, and operation. Mastery of the model only comes when they are played in combination. It is here, among the complex harmonies of *community, land* and *trust*, that a song of transformation is most likely to be heard in the places people call home. The music is in the spaces, boys and girls; the music is in the spaces.

Notes

1. These variations extend to the manner in which the CLT itself is characterized. Many practitioners employ terms like "strategy," "mechanism," "vehicle," or "platform" when describing the CLT. I have done the same, sometimes using these terms interchangeably with "model." My use of the last is not meant to champion model as the best of these terms. It is merely to follow the custom that began in 1972 with the first book about the CLT, which called it "a new model for land tenure in America."

2. This is hardly the first time I've bemoaned (and ridiculed) the readiness to discard this component of the "classic" CLT whenever funders, bankers, or practitioners consider community landholding and long-term ground leasing to be "too difficult." See, for example: "Ground Leasing Without Tears," *Shelterforce Weekly,* January 29, 2014. Available at: *https://shelterforce.org/2014/01/29/ground_leasing_without_tears/*

3. An early attempt to develop a theory of the formation and interaction of these "property interest groups" can be found in J.E. Davis, *Contested Ground: Collective Action and the Urban Neighborhood* (Ithaca, NY: Cornell University Press, 1991).

4. Adam Gopnik, "Wired: What Alexander Calder Set in Motion." *The New Yorker* (December 4, 2017: 73–77).

5. A more detailed argument for the transformative potential of the "classic" CLT can be found in J.E. Davis, "Common Ground: Community-Owned Land as a Platform for Equitable and Sustainable Development." *University of San Francisco Law Review* 51 (1), 2017. Thoughtful critiques of this argument, addressing the question of whether nonmarket models of ownership are, in fact, "politically transformative," appear in James DeFilippis, *Unmaking Goliath: Community Control in the Face of Global Capital* (Routledge, 2004) and his more recent essay, "On the Transformative Potential of Community Land Trusts in the United States," co-authored with Olivia R. Williams, Joseph Pierce, Deborah G. Martin, Rich Kruger, and Azadeh Hadizadeh Esfahani. *Antipode* (February 12, 2019).

6. An online archive of materials about the Appalachian Student Health Coalition is part of the Southern Historical Collection at the University of North Carolina (*www.coalition. web.unc.edu*).

ABOUT THE CONTRIBUTORS

LINE ALGOED is a PhD researcher at Cosmopolis, Center for Urban Research at the Vrije Universiteit in Brussels and a Research Fellow at the International Institute of Social Studies in The Hague. She works with the Caño Martín Peña CLT in Puerto Rico on international exchanges among communities involved in land struggles. She is also an Associate at the Center for CLT Innovation. Previously, Line was a World Habitat Awards Program Manager at BSHF (now World Habitat). She holds an MA in Cultural Anthropology from the University of Leiden and an MA in Sociology from the London School of Economics.

YVES CABANNES (y.cabannes@ucl.ac.uk) is an urban specialist, activist and scholar. Over the past forty years he has been involved in research and development on urban issues, people-led initiatives, and local democracy with NGOs and local governments in Asia, Latin America, Africa and the Middle East. Since the early 1990s, he has supported, researched, taught, and advocated for participatory budgeting and planning, urban agriculture, community land trusts, and housing rights in different regions of the world and has published widely on these topics. He became Emeritus Professor of Development Planning at the University College London/Development Planning Unit in 2015.

JOHN EMMEUS DAVIS is a founding partner of Burlington Associates in Community Development, a national consulting cooperative. He was housing director in Burlington, Vermont under Mayors Bernie Sanders and Peter Clavelle. Community land trusts have been a prominent part of his professional practice and scholarly writing for nearly 40 years. His publications include *Contested Ground* (1991), *The Affordable City* (1994), *The City-CLT Partnership* (2008), *The Community Land Trust Reader* (2010), and *Manuel d'antispéculation immobilière* (2014). He co-produced the film, *Arc of Justice,* and is co-director of the Center for CLT Innovation (*https://cltweb.org*). He holds an MS and PhD from Cornell University.

María E. Hernández-Torrales holds an LLM in environmental law from the Vermont Law School and an MA in Business Education from New York University. She studied for her undergraduate and Juris Doctor degrees at the University of Puerto Rico. Since 2005 she has been doing pro bono legal work for the Proyecto ENLACE and for the Fideicomiso de la Tierra del Caño Martín Peña. Since 2008, Hernández-Torrales has worked as an attorney and clinical professor at the University of Puerto Rico School of Law where she teaches the Community Economic Development Clinic.

David Ireland is Chief Executive of World Habitat, a UK-based international housing charity that helps to scale up solutions to the world's housing problems, from slum upgrading to post-disaster housing and homelessness. His organization also operates the World Habitat Awards in partnership with UN-Habitat, and runs programmes aimed at ending homelessness and scaling up community-led housing. David is trustee of Action Homeless and was previously CEO of the Empty Homes Agency where he persuaded successive UK governments to introduce legislation and to fund programmes to get empty homes into use. He was awarded OBE in 2013 for services to housing.

Steve King is Executive Director of the Oakland Community Land Trust in Oakland, California (*https://oakclt.org*). He has spent the past 15 years working for community-based organizations in the areas of equitable development, affordable housing, and applied social research. Steve previously served as the Housing and Economic Development Coordinator at the Urban Strategies Council, also based in Oakland. He holds a MS in Urban Planning from Columbia University, and a BA in Environmental Science from Boston University.

Verena Lenna is an architect and urbanist (PhD at IUAV and KU Leuven). Through her work and research, she explores the relationship between emancipation and the living environment. Whether design-based or not, her projects and collaborations are mainly action-oriented and community-based. She has focused on themes such as labour conditions, arts, and culture. More recently, she has worked on property, looking at the role of the design process in the realisation of Brussels Community Land Trust projects. She is a co-founder and member of Commons Josaphat, a collective created to transform a 24-hectare site in Brussels for the common good.

Jerry Maldonado is Director of the Cities and States Program at the Ford Foundation. He joined Ford in the aftermath of Hurricanes Katrina and Rita, overseeing the Foundation's Gulf Coast Transformation Initiative. Over the past decade he has developed and managed several of the Foundation's national, regional, and state grant-making initiatives, working at the intersection of equitable development and civic engagement.

Prior to Ford, Jerry worked with the Rockefeller Brothers Fund, Carnegie Council on Ethics and International Affairs, and the United Nations Non-Governmental Liaison Service. He has a master's degree from Columbia University and a bachelor's degree from Brown University.

PHILIP ROSS (rosspe97@gmail.com) is the former Mayor of Letchworth Garden City and is the current Chairman of the New Garden Cities Alliance, an organization that champions the social goals of the Garden City Movement. He is an international speaker on Garden Cities and, together with Yves Cabannes, wrote the book *21st Century Garden Cities of To-Morrow — A Manifesto.* He still lives in Letchworth and is married with three children. He works as a freelance business analyst.

www.ingramcontent.com/pod-product-compliance
Lightning Source LLC
Chambersburg PA
CBHW080600030426
42336CB00019B/3273